Praise for *Privileged Spaces*

'*Privileged Spaces* expertly explores how evolving university estates ~~influence~~ the demands placed on library spaces. Highlighting the critical intersection of space retention, service delivery and user satisfaction, this book shows how vital it is for library, estates and facilities leaders to collaborate effectively.

By examining the challenges of flexible space design, this insightful work provides a guide for navigating change in library environments, ensuring that spaces evolve in harmony with university planning. A must-read for anyone involved in shaping the future of academic libraries and their services.'

Ayub Khan FCLIP MBE, Director of Designing Libraries and Head of Warwickshire Libraries and Culture

'*Privileged Spaces* is a timely book dealing with the sometimes fraught path for library managers in universities, who have to demonstrate the need for continuing physical space for the library service, when universities wish to expand and achieve this by either limiting or curtailing the library's footprint. Regina Everitt and Neil Everitt use their individual experience in both libraries and facilities management in the UK university sector, together with thoughtful contributions from fellow academics, to bring together a resource text that will serve the range of stakeholders in the academic sector. Much of the content will support library managers in other sectors too, especially public and workplace libraries, offering useful practical examples for the readership.'

Stella Thebridge, co-author of *Better by Design*, 2nd edition (Facet Publishing)

Privileged Spaces

Privileged Spaces

Academic Libraries in University
Estates Strategy

Edited by
Regina Everitt and Neil Everitt

facet
publishing

© This compilation: Regina Everitt and Neil Everitt 2025
The chapters: the contributors 2025

Published by Facet Publishing
c/o British Library, 96 Euston Road, London NW1 2DB
www.facetpublishing.co.uk

Facet Publishing is wholly owned by CILIP: the Library and Information
Association.

British Library Cataloguing in Publication Data
A catalogue record for this book is available from the British Library.

ISBN 978-1-78330-646-6 (paperback)
ISBN 978-1-78330-647-3 (hardback)
ISBN 978-1-78330-648-0 (PDF)
ISBN 978-1-78330-649-7 (EPUB)

First published 2025

Typeset from editors' files in 10.5/13 Revival 565 and Frutiger by
Flagholme Publishing Services.
Printed and made in Great Britain by CPI Group (UK) Ltd, Croydon,
CR0 4YY.

Contents

Figures and Tables

Notes on Contributors

Editors

Neil Everitt is Director of Strategic Engagement at the Institute of Workplace and Facilities Management (IWFM). Before joining IWFM he developed an interest in property after completing a volunteer procurement project for a charity providing community-based services in London. Prior to that he fulfilled a number of sales and marketing, procurement and change management roles, in several countries, with a large multinational mining organisation.

Regina Everitt is Assistant Chief Operating Officer and Director of Library, Archives and Learning Services at the University of East London. She started her career as a technical author/trainer in software development companies in the US and UK. She transitioned into the higher education sector developing and managing libraries, social learning spaces and other learning resources. Concerned about the low representation of Global Ethnic Majority leaders in academic libraries, she works with the sector to develop more diverse talent. She co-edited *Narrative Expansions: Interpreting Decolonisation in Academic Libraries* (Facet Publishing, 2021), which considers how libraries are navigating this contested topic.

Contributors

Dr Melanie Benson Marshall is a post-doctoral researcher at the Information School, University of Sheffield. She is currently a post-doctoral research associate on the project 'VOICES: The Value of Openness, Inclusion, Communication, and Engagement for Science in a post-pandemic world'.

Lucy Black, MSc, FIWFM, FRSA, is Associate Director – Facilities and Student Accommodation at the University of Plymouth, delivering in-house and outsourced services. She is chair of the Association of University Directors of Estates Strategic FM group, leading a group representing facilities managers across the UK's higher education sector. With 30 years' experience in facilities management, Lucy has previously held similar roles in university, local authority and charity sectors, leading and developing teams and services. She is a Fellow of the Institute of Workplace and Facilities Management, where she was a non-executive director, chair of Members' Council and chaired the Sustainability Special Interest Group.

Becky Bradshaw has worked in higher education for over 20 years, taking her current position as Chief Operating Officer at the University of Northampton in 2023. Becky led the operationalisation of the University's new and innovative Waterside Campus and directed their strategic response to the coronavirus pandemic. She is passionate about social impact and the influence of professional services on student outcomes, alongside sustainability and environmental improvement, and has led development of both the University's sustainability and estates strategies. She is secretary to the Association of University Directors of Estates and often contributes to sector-wide working and advisory groups.

Dr Jennifer A. Burnham is a senior university teacher in the Department of Chemistry, University of Sheffield. She completed an MEd in Teaching and Learning in Higher Education at the University of Sheffield in 2012, is a University of Sheffield Senate Award winner for Excellence in Learning and Teaching and is a Principal Fellow of the Higher Education Academy.

Leo Care is a senior university teacher in the School of Architecture, University of Sheffield. He is currently the Year 3 undergraduate programme leader and co-director of Live Works, the first university-led urban room in the UK. He is also a Director of Chiles Evans + Care Architects, and co-founder of the Open House Project Cohousing group.

Chris Clow is product manager (On Campus Education), IT Services, University of Sheffield. His specialities are: IT/AV equipment trainer, technical support, developing resources and improving the learning experience for students through inquiry-based learning.

Dr Andrew Cox is a senior lecturer at the Information School, University of Sheffield. He wrote the *Drivers for the Usage of SCONUL Member Libraries* SCONUL research report (June 2021), with Dr Benson Marshall. Much of his research relates to the information professions and their response to contemporary trends such as artificial intelligence, datafication, managerialism and the perceived crisis in well-being.

John Cox writes about and analyses issues impacting on academic libraries and their positioning. He retired as University Librarian at the University of Galway in November 2023 and is currently writing a book on *The Position and Strategic Positioning of Academic Libraries: Global Drivers and Local Politics*, to be published by Facet Publishing. His most recent published work is a two-part SWOT analysis of academic libraries in the *New Review of*

Academic Librarianship. Previous publications include review articles on the higher education environment driving academic library strategy, positioning the academic library in the institution, and communicating library roles in digital scholarship.

Savannah Hanson was Education Officer at University of Sheffield Students' Union.

Dr Tim Herrick is a senior university teacher in the School of Education, University of Sheffield. He is currently Director of Student Voice, Faculty of Social Sciences. He is a Senior Fellow of the Higher Education Academy (FHEA), University of Sheffield Senate Award Fellow and was FindAMasters.com Masters Teacher of the Year, 2023.

Dr Myles Jones is a senior lecturer in the Department of Psychology, University of Sheffield. He is a member of the Neuroscience and Cognition research group. He is a Senior Fellow of the Higher Education Academy (FHEA) and a University of Sheffield Senate Fellow of Learning and Teaching Excellence.

Robert Kilpatrick is a seasoned estates professional and qualified building services engineer with over 25 years' experience within the higher education sector. During this time he has managed large estates teams, having responsibility for delivering hard and soft facilities management services and capital development. He has extensive experience of acting as project director/manager for large capital projects, including complex infrastructure district energy heating networks. He is currently an assistant director of estates at University of Strathclyde. He is also a board member of the National Library of Scotland and an external examiner for the BEng Building Services course at Glasgow Caledonian University.

Alison Lahlafi is Associate Director: Chief Librarian at University of Bradford and has worked in university libraries across Yorkshire and Kent. Alison has a life-long interest in providing inclusive and accessible library services and has previously led on developing library support for international students at Sheffield Hallam University library. She was a founder member of both the Open Rose Group supporting people with disabilities at eight university libraries across Yorkshire and the YHULISS group – Yorkshire and Humberside University Librarians' Inclusive Student Support Group.

Alison Little is Associate Director, Learning Strategy and Student Engagement, the Library, University of Sheffield. She leads the Library Information Advisory Team, the Library Learning and Teaching Services Team, the Content and Collections Team, and Study Space Development and Library Estates Planning. She also represents the Library on the Research Libraries UK Collections Strategy Network and is a member of the Academic Libraries North Associate Directors Network.

Anna O'Neill is the University Librarian at the University of Warwick. She has held professional roles in libraries for over 30 years and has a range of experience across a number of sectors, including the National Health Service, heritage, charities, law and financial services. Over her career she has written many business cases (learning more from the failures than the successes) for both library refurbishment projects and new builds.

Chris Powis is Director of Library, Learning and Student Services at the University of Northampton, where he has worked in a number of roles since joining the then Nene College as the Business and Law Librarian over 30 years ago. He is a National Teaching Fellow and a Fellow of CILIP and the Royal Society of Arts. His professional interests include learning spaces and the role of professional services in learning and teaching, and has written and spoken widely on these issues.

Tim Wales is University Librarian at Cranfield University, UK. He has previously led libraries at Brunel University London, Rothamsted Research, the University of West London and London Business School. He completed his MSc in Information Science at City St George's, University of London. Tim has written on many professional topics, including library strategy, business librarianship and library technologies and edited his first book, *Business School Libraries in the 21st Century* in 2014. He is a chartered member of CILIP, a fellow of the Higher Education Academy and an editorial board member of the *New Review of Academic Librarianship*.

Introduction: A Meeting of the Founders of Library Science and Facilities Management

Regina Everitt and Neil Everitt

The growing organism

A library is a growing organism. This is the fifth law of library science as defined by Shiyali Ramamrita Ranganathan, a librarian and mathematician who is considered to be the founder of library science. In his seminal work, *Five Laws of Library Science*, Ranganathan defined core principles for librarianship: (1) books are for use; (2) every person his or her book; (3) every book its reader; (4) save time for the reader; and (5) a library is a growing organism (Ranganathan, 2006). Although originally published in 1931, the work remains largely relevant today, with 'book' interpreted as any physical or digital library resource and the 'growing organism' as a physical or virtual space.

This book focuses on the physical space as contemplated in Ranganathan's work. The fifth law considers the management of the inevitable growth of physical stock, the fixtures and fittings to contain it, the systems to track it, the reading rooms for the service users and the workspace for the library staff. The library leader of today has the same considerations, with the role of the library and its space continuing to transform in order to meet the evolving demands of users, ranging from access to books, to use of technologies, to keeping warm in cold weather.

Ranganathan's fifth law is non-contentious when funds are available to feed the 'growing organism' and allow it to 'take . . . in new matter . . . change in size, and take new shapes and forms' (Ranganathan, 2006). But imagine evoking this law in a university estates strategy meeting today where conversations may be focused on constrained spaces, limited funding and competing priorities:

> We're growing, so we need to rethink how we are using space across the university estate – and that includes the library!

Do students even use all these books? We need to create more teaching spaces.

Students are using information online, so let's add more study spaces, PCs or plug points and get rid of some of this shelving.

Library buildings or spaces that have been developed with funding given on the condition that they must be used for library purposes are exempt from this debate, regardless of any estate master plan. However, the university library is an estate asset. As the repository of information and source of knowledge, the library can be perceived as a privileged space – a haven to think, explore the wonders of rich collections, seek solace or simply meet friends. And yet it is as much an estate asset as any other office space. Library leaders with discrete buildings or spaces independent of teaching rooms, other services or links to centralised booking systems may take another view. However, as institutions must adapt their strategy in response to internal and external pressures for financial stability (e.g., increase or decrease in student numbers), these privileged library spaces are coming under increased scrutiny as the estate strategy is developed to deliver institutional aims.

Library leaders must work in partnership with the estates and facilities team to ensure that the space and services align with the university strategy while protecting the student experience. So, they must be involved at the earliest stages of estates master planning, particularly when discussions and decisions about library spaces are taking place.

Some definitions
The composition of estates and facilities teams differs across organisations. For the purposes of this Introduction, estates and facilities generally refer to the directorate that manages and maintains university estates assets. For simplicity, *estates projects* refers to the team that manages refurbishments and major construction projects. The project team may also include architects, designers, space managers, construction engineers, etc. *Facilities management* refers to the teams that manage services, from soft services such as customer services and cleaning to hard services such as plumbing and the building environment (e.g., centralised heating and air handling). Library leaders with responsibility for leading services in library buildings will need to work closely with estates and facilities teams to ensure that the building is functional, safe and suitable for the services delivered.

Managing the growing organism
Some 30 years after the publication of Ranganathan's *Five Laws*, American businessman Ross Perot was said to have coined the term *facilities manage-*

ment as he contemplated the management of systems and technology within offices (Wiggins, 2020). Planning and consideration were needed for how to house and maintain the large, physical computing systems that powered the 'modern' office spaces of the time. Had the technological revolution reached Ranganathan's library in his time, his fifth law would certainly have applied, as these systems would have been integral to managing library records, transactions and other information. Of course, during Perot's day many services were hosted on office premises, whereas today many such services are in the 'cloud'.

Twenty years later, in the early 1980s in the United Kingdom (UK), British architect and space planner Francis Duffy and colleagues teamed up with information technology (IT) consultants and social scientists to consider how people, organisations and technology influence decision making around building design. The *ORBIT* reports (*Office Research: Buildings and Information Technology*) provided frameworks for assessing the current and future demands of buildings to enable their sustainable use (Duffy et al., 1985).

Although both Perot and Duffy have been considered the founders of facilities management, Duffy's advocacy for facilities managers to understand 'user expectations' for spaces rather than to opt for 'ease of delivery' (McLennan, 2012) articulates the importance of the relationship between the library leader and the estates and facilities teams. In the *ORBIT-2* report, Duffy and colleagues defined 'high coordination' of facilities planners with 'high involvement' of impacted staff as the strategy for organisations concerned about employee satisfaction and retention (Duffy et al., 1985). Duffy et al. understood that user engagement and satisfaction are integral to planning and delivery, rather than 'the single point of view' from estates and facilities that 'can lead to delivery of poor outcomes' (Duffy et al., 1985).

Ranganathan in his time would have been a formidable stakeholder for his organisation's estates and facilities team. In *Five Laws of Library Science*, he writes in intimate detail how the architecture of the library must accommodate the book racks of a specific height and weight (which he designed, incidentally), and even describes the look of the shelf labels. Had Duffy been the architect and space planner for Madras University Library, where Ranganathan was librarian, he no doubt would have engaged Ranganathan in design decisions. One could imagine that Ranganathan would have had it no other way!

The extent to which the library leader can be involved in discussions or influence decisions about university estate strategy may depend on their proximity to the decision-making table (e.g., member of university management board). A reductive view of their involvement with the estates and facilities team may be around routine maintenance or refurbishment. Where estates project teams may make decisions about new builds or larger projects, the involvement of the library team may be restricted to colour palettes or furnishings. Even Ranganathan referred to 'library authorities', suggesting some decision-making entity beyond his own (Ranganathan, 2006). Whatever the involvement of the library leader or team, it is useful to understand what questions to ask of estates project teams, because once the building project is completed the library team will be the first-line support for dealing with the day-to-day operations of the 'organism'.

About the book

This book was conceived after discussions with library leaders who were navigating impacts to library spaces due to university growth strategies. For some leaders this meant expansion of library spaces or even new buildings. For others it meant loss of space and/or investment to prioritise teaching or other activities. In many cases, some library leaders had little experience of bidding for or working on major building projects and were keen to share experiences. At the time of the writing of this book, there were several building projects underway with library leaders so steeped in project delivery that they were unable to contribute to this work. However, from discussions with some of these leaders, the themes and experiences discussed in the chapters in this book will resonate.

The contributions in this book are from leaders in institutions in the UK and Ireland although international perspectives were sought. However, the discussions about influencing institutional strategy, developing a compelling business case and working effectively with estates and facilities teams, illustrated by case studies about project delivery, will yield universal lessons.

What becomes clear in this work is the cruciality of a good working relationship between the library and estates and facilities teams. They must work in partnership to develop and maintain safe and sustainable facilities to meet the learning, teaching and research aims of universities and their staff and students. In this book there are some great examples of teams working together to deliver innovative solutions. And there are examples of challenges, especially where there are competing views about investment and impacts on service delivery and the student experience. Like Ranganathan, the library leader will seek to guard and nurture the 'growing organism', working in partnership with estates and facilities teams who, like Duffy, value stakeholder input.

This collection is divided into two sections: Part 1 Foundations and Part 2 Landings. Part 1 discusses the roles, relationships and interdependencies of the library and the estates and facilities teams. It discusses the value of libraries in selling universities, making the case for why the two services must work in partnership to deliver university strategy. It also provides a primer for writing compelling business cases to advocate for investment in libraries as part of the university estates master plan. Part 1 concludes with a discussion about libraries through a 'workplace' lens, foregrounding the people and the activities that take place within the spaces and how facilities management professionals take a strategic view in delivering solutions in collaboration with stakeholders. Part 2 brings to life the themes discussed in Part 1 through four case studies ranging from delivering large, complex building projects to smaller space enhancements that have significant, positive impact on the student experience.

Part 1

In Chapter 1 Black and Kilpatrick define the role of facilities management in ensuring spaces' regulatory compliance, safety and security. They also discuss the role of the estates projects team and how an efficient handover can mitigate some of the challenges around snagging and other issues at project closure.

In Chapter 2 Wales discusses how the position of the library leader within the university structure impacts on their ability to influence decisions about university strategy. Drawing on feedback from directors about their experiences, he concludes that library leaders need to continually 'lobby' to ensure that they get the investment needed for their services.

In Chapter 3 Regina Everitt discusses tools for evidence gathering to influence decision making, such as utilisation and occupancy measures, surveys and other qualitative methods. She illustrates how an imbalance in the 'project management triangle' could impact on project outcomes. Later, in Chapter 5, she illustrates the role the library plays in selling the university to prospective students and how the perception of value can change over the students' time at the university. She also highlights the need for library leaders to sell this value internally or risk being overlooked in budget and estate master planning.

In Chapter 4 O'Neill provides a primer on developing a compelling business case to influence university strategy, drawing on her experience. She also emphasises the importance of gaining support from key partners such as IT and estates and facilities teams to influence executive-level decision making.

In Chapter 6 Neil Everitt shares views on workplace and facilities management development and its role in delivering university strategy through effective stakeholder engagement and change management.

Part 2

In Chapter 7 Lahlafi provides a case study of a high-impact space enhancement to deliver an inclusive space for students with children. The study illustrates the numerous practical considerations to be addressed even for projects that are considered 'small scale,' including changes to existing university policies.

In Chapter 8 John Cox discusses the commitment and tenacity involved in advocating for the planning of a learning commons building over a 25-year period. His study illustrates the importance of laying the 'political' foundations before the first brick is laid.

In Chapter 9 Bradshaw and Powis describe the ambitious redevelopment of a campus that involved a change in pedagogy and a new way of working, considered radical by some stakeholders. Their study illustrates how a good working relationship between the library and estates and facilities teams yielded successful delivery of the university strategy.

Drawing on their research on what students at the University of Sheffield value in informal and social learning spaces, in Chapter 10 Andrew Cox and colleagues discuss the inclusivity of spaces and whether the needs of certain student communities are left unaddressed. Their research findings would usefully inform any estates master planning.

Acknowledgement and thanks

We thank all the authors for sharing their stories and experiences, which will be invaluable for leaders navigating similar territory while delivering on institutional strategy. A lot of the information shared in these pages has been learned 'on the job' and written in the throes of a tight deadline! Hopefully, the lessons learned will go some way to assist library and estates and facilities leaders in building good working relationships.

References

Duffy, F., Davis, G., Becker, F. and Sims, W. (1985) *Executive Overview: An Overview of the Main Volumes of the ORBIT-2 Project and Rating Process on Organizations, Buildings and Information Technology*, Harbinger Group Inc.

McLennan, P. (2012) FM World Interview: Frank Duffy (CBE) and Peter McLennan, *Facilitate*, March, 1–17.

Ranganathan, S. R. (2006 [1931]) *The Five Laws of Library Science*, Ess Ess Publications.

Wiggins, J. (2020) *Facilities Manager's Desk Reference, 3rd Edition*, John Wiley & Sons Ltd.

Part 1 Foundations

1

Estates and Facilities with Libraries: Working Together to Deliver University Strategy

Lucy Black and Robert Kilpatrick

Introduction

This chapter considers how colleagues in estates and facilities and library directorates work together to ensure the provision of high-quality and fit-for-purpose library facilities for students and staff. University libraries are regarded as a key service provision for students and the library aligns with the institution's strategic vision, mission and values in providing an excellent student experience, delivering operational excellence and supporting learning, teaching and research. Libraries are well recognised as being one of the key considerations when students are making university choices. The requirement to comply with legislation, particularly in relation to safety, is the bedrock of service delivery, while enabling a positive experience for all library users. Estates and facilities and library teams are both critical in delivering an excellent customer experience.

Estates and facilities teams have responsibilities across the whole university estate and need to prioritise the allocation of their staff and financial resources, taking all areas into account when considering repairs, maintenance and capital projects as well as provision of services. It is for library teams to develop elements of capital business cases for improvements to the library, explaining the benefits of proposed changes, and working with estates and facilities, who will contribute their understanding of the technical aspects and costs. Both capital and ongoing revenue implications need to be included in such business cases, with sufficient allocations being agreed before submission to the relevant governance and finance committees for approval before works can proceed. Both teams should have regular meetings with a clear agenda that covers operational and development activities, should work together to respond to changing priorities in university strategy, and need to interpret how this is reflected in physical infrastructure and service provision.

Facilities management

Facilities management (FM) is the 'organizational function which integrates people, place and process within the built environment with the purpose of improving the quality of life of people and the productivity of the core business' (EUROFM, 2024). This incorporates a wide range of activities to ensure

- compliance with legal requirements;
- the day-to-day safety of the premises and people using it;
- maintenance to protect the building over the long term; and
- the building's availability for the specified users and services.

While FM is generally focused on managing existing buildings, it may take the lead on works to upgrade, change and improve existing spaces and to construct new buildings.

FM is often described as being either *hard* or *soft*. One way to view the split is by thinking of what would happen if you could turn a building upside down and shake it; what you would be left with after things have fallen out are likely to be considered hard FM responsibilities, while the activities that have separated from the structure of the building rest with soft FM.

Facilities management in United Kingdom (UK) universities

FM teams work in partnership with the library to provide a safe, attractive and welcoming physical learning environment. A wide range of activities contributes to this, and the majority of FM services will be provided by a directorate charged with these responsibilities. This may be called Estates, Estates and Facilities, Campus Services, etc. The structure of these directorates varies across the sector; some functions, such as catering, may sit in other areas. In broad terms, the structure is often based on the main functions: soft FM, hard FM and capital development.

Soft FM focuses on providing services which enable the library to function. These may include:

- cleaning;
- recycling and waste management;
- security services, e.g., security officers patrolling and emergency response to incidents;
- access control system management – producing of university cards, changing access; rights of individuals, groups of staff and students or of doors and areas of the library;
- mail and courier services;

- portering and moving;
- grounds maintenance;
- pest control;
- catering.

Hard FM involves management of the structure of the building, including but not limited to the following:

- mechanical and electrical systems
  - mains power supply
  - lighting systems
  - security systems, e.g., intruder alarms, CCTV, access control
  - IT server rooms, cabling for IT systems
  - lightning protection
  - generators for power back-up.
- heating, ventilation and air conditioning (HVAC)
  - natural and mechanical ventilation
  - air conditioning
  - boilers
  - drinking water
- life-safe systems
  - emergency lighting
  - fire alarms
  - call systems for people with disabilities
  - refuge panels
  - gas detection
- water hygiene
  - sewage and drainage
  - water for drinking
- maintenance and repair of fabric of the building (from loose handles to re-roofing)
- lifts and escalators
- plumbing (toilets, sinks)
- power
  - electricity supply
  - heating power supply.

Capital development leads on the development of new library spaces, covering projects from full-scale new buildings through to minor works in existing premises.

Operational facilities management

Legislative requirements

The university has to ensure that robust systems and processes are in place to ensure that legal obligations relating to the library buildings are met. This will include having nominated duty holders for a range of specific hazards, e.g., legionella. If things are not managed appropriately, people's safety can be compromised. Depending on the nature of any impact from hazards, there is a risk to the university's reputation and, potentially, heavy fines from the Health & Safety Executive or courts. Accident and incident investigations take time and, if nothing else, will require staff resources to carry out. All or part of the library could have to be shut depending on what has occurred.

Staff in estates and facilities teams are likely to be the duty holders for many of the regulations, having the necessary training and accreditation to fulfil these roles. It is generally considered to be part of their professional role and may be included in specific job roles. Whoever is the identified responsible person will need to keep up to date with the legislation and maintain good records of ongoing training. Should there be a need for the university to demonstrate compliance, evidence of such would be required.

It is possible to appoint an external contractor to carry out some of the duties required to ensure compliance, e.g., water testing in the case of legionella. It is important to note that responsibility cannot be delegated to a contractor, but by appointing someone who is considered competent and responding to their findings, the university would be in a strong position if anything went wrong.

For FM, ensuring legislative compliance is the priority. Budget allocations will be focused on this before other aspects of operating the building are considered.

Table 1.1 opposite lists some of the legislation that is relevant to library facilities management (Wiggins, 2014).

Delivery of services

FM services may be delivered by in-house teams, where staff are directly employed by the university, by external contractors working under contracts managed by university staff (known as outsourcing) or by a combination of these. Services which all universities will outsource include waste disposal, while most will use specialist contractors for at least some activities. The range of specialisms would require an unfeasibly large in-house team, with some needed only occasionally.

Some universities outsource their FM services through large contracts. Management of these contracts remains with the university, but the day-today interactions for library staff may be with managers and staff from the external company.

Table 1.1 *Legislation relevant to library facilities management*

Equality	Equalities Act 2010 Can all staff and students access the library and services? Is there a need for physical adaptations or for alternative methods of service delivery?
Health and safety Ensuring the building is safe for staff, students and visitors and that any contractors working in it are operating safely	The Health and Safety at Work Act 1974 is the underlying legislation. Some of the regulations are: • Control of Asbestos Regulations 2006 • If building or maintenance works are being done on the building, they could disturb asbestos that has been safely encapsulated. E.g., drilling into a wall to put up a picture could damage a surface and expose asbestos. The university's asbestos register should be accessed by anyone carrying out works to confirm that their activities can be done safely. • Electricity at Work Regulations 1989 • Gas Safety (Installation and Equipment) 1998 • Control of Substances Hazardous to Health Regulations 2002 E.g., chemical used by the cleaning team • The Control of Legionella Bacteria in Water Systems – HSE Approved Code of Practice for taps in toilets, tea points and water fountains
Environmental protection	The Environment Protection Act 1990 is the underlying legislation. Some of the relevant regulations are: • Waste Management Regulations 1996 • Waste Electrical and Electronic Equipment Directive (WEEE)
Fire Ensuring the building, its contents and occupants are protected from fire	The Regulatory Reform (Fire Safety) Order 2005 covers fire risk assessments, appropriate detection and firefighting equipment, signage, training, provision of fire marshals. Responsibilities may be split between different teams in the university, e.g., a fire officer in a health and safety team; FM for provision and maintenance of detection and alarm systems; library staff for daily checks that fire exits and routes are clear, fire marshals.
Food Where catering is provided in the library	Food Safety Act 1990 and a series of associated regulations

Hard FM in the library

The main interaction between hard FM services and the library is through maintenance activities. These may be planned, known as planned preventative maintenance (PPM), or as a result of faults that require rectification, known as reactive maintenance.

Planned preventative maintenance. Hard FM services such as the lighting systems or plumbing require regular servicing and maintenance to ensure that they continue to work effectively and to maximise their functional lives. Some maintenance may be a statutory requirement or be demanded by the university insurers. Examples of this are fire protection systems and lift maintenance, where the impact of poorly maintained systems could be catastrophic. Some items may be on a regular cycle, for example annual servicing of lifts, while others may be added to the PPM schedule for the year, having been identified as requiring work.

Library and FM teams should work together on the timing of PPM to understand and minimise the impact on users. It is not possible for all works to be carried out during the summer period from July to September, when the library may have reduced activity. The overall amount of work that needs to be done both in the library and across the university estate means that suitable contractors would not have capacity, and FM teams also need to be able to manage it all effectively. Ways to mitigate impacts can be considered, e.g., advance communication to users, signposting to alternative social learning spaces.

Reactive maintenance is required when something has occurred that affects the building in such a way that work is needed to restore operations. Examples include leaks or flooding, lighting failures, broken door handles, and can range from those requiring urgent attention through to others with a lower priority. There will be a process within the university for library staff to report any problems they find, such as a helpdesk or similar. The reporting process enables all issues to be logged and actions to be tracked. Even a simple system will enable data analysis of types of fault, locations, etc., which will help the FM teams to identify patterns, e.g., a product that is failing, a location that may need a different solution.

Repairs will be prioritised by the FM team and may be given an associated numerical rating. This will take into account an assessment of the impact on the library's performance, safety and compliance. The impact refers to the potential consequences of not fixing the problem, such as damage to stock or the building, injury to staff, students or visitors, or non-compliance with statutory requirements. The urgency will also be taken into account, considering the severity of the problem, the availability of alternative solutions, the demand for the affected service or space and the expectations of library users.

FM teams should ensure that assessment of priority includes any factors specific to the library, separately from any incidents.

The prioritisation of a reported fault should be communicated to the library team, and updates on progress provided where appropriate. The criteria used to determine priorities and associated response times should be understood by library teams, and should include any specific factors that are relevant to the library. In some universities formal service level agreements (SLAs) may be in place. These can help in defining response times, but can make the relationship between teams less collaborative and potentially more antagonistic, as staff will rely on a predetermined set of responses rather than working together on solutions. Depending on the seriousness of the event, FM and library teams will need to work together to manage the situation, with FM focusing on the building-related issue and library on mitigations for users. Emergency response is discussed later in this section.

Soft FM services
Cleaning

The FM team is responsible for cleaning the library, including floors, furniture and toilets. Hygiene is the priority, so if staffing is low for any reason, toilets and kitchen/tea points will be the primary focus. Consumables such as toilet paper, soap and paper towels (if provided) need to be kept stocked. With 24/7 use of library buildings, FM teams must work around students and staff, and so discussion with library teams about the best time of day for noisy activities such as vacuum cleaning will help to minimise disruption.

Specialist cleaning of book stacks may be managed by either library or FM teams, with external or internal staff used for this infrequent task. It is not usually considered as part of a standard cleaning contract, due to the need to understand the specific requirements.

Depending on the level of use of the library, it may be necessary to restock consumables during the day. There are often close links between cleaning and library staff, for example, early-morning cleaners may be aware of students who are sleeping in the library or are struggling in other ways and can inform library staff, who will take relevant action as defined by the institution's policies.

Waste and recycling

Waste will be collected from the library by the FM team. Appropriate bins will be provided to enable items to be split into different waste streams to help maximise recycling. Where larger collections are needed, e.g., packaging from library purchases, special arrangements may be in place requiring contact with the FM team. Emptying bins and removal of waste may be done by the cleaning team as part of their regime. At certain times of the year additional collections may be needed to ensure that bins are not overflowing.

Provision and emptying of sanitary hygiene bins from female and gender-neutral toilets will usually be done by external contractors. University strategy regarding provision of gender-neutral facilities has increased the number of units being serviced, with concomitant additional costs. This is a small example of the impact of strategy on services.

Security

Maintaining the safety of people and of stock is done through a combination of inputs. Access control systems, with people needing valid university identification to enter spaces, provide an initial barrier. However, where access is permitted to non-university people, other arrangements might be in place to afford them entry while maintaining control. These may be part of the wider university access control systems managed by FM, or a standalone system managed by the library. Changes to access rights will be managed by the system owner, as well as door opening and locking times.

Useful data can be produced from access control systems, such as the numbers of people entering at different times, from which faculties, etc. No access-control system can provide complete protection from non-authorised entry into the building. Other systems may also be in place, monitored by security teams or available for review after incidents; these could include CCTV and intruder alarms.

University security patrollers may come through the library building while it is open; this will be down to local arrangements and capacity. Discussions may result in additional patrols at specific times of year when it is known that issues occur. Library and security teams can agree on approaches, with staff working together to resolve issues. Security teams are increasingly providing support for students, particularly at times of day when very few other staff are on campus but the library may still be open. In addition to regular patrolling, security officers will respond to incidents (threat, fire, flood, etc.). Library staff should have contact numbers easily available.

Mail and courier services

Incoming and outgoing mail and packages will go through the university post room. This will include interlibrary loans as well as other printed materials. The FM team may provide internal delivery services, with items being taken between different sites if there are libraries in more than one location. If material is stored off site, collection and delivery services may sit with FM, with agreed procedures with the library. Some universities offer postal loans of printed materials. Suitable packaging will be done by the library team and dispatch will be done by the FM postal services, ensuring that costs are covered and allocated appropriately.

Portering and moving

Minor moves of furniture and other items in the library may need assistance from the FM portering team. Larger moves which are part of projects may be done by the in-house team, or external contractors.

Pest control

All buildings are subject to colonisation by animals in ways that may cause damage or hygiene issues. These may be rodents, insects or birds. The best form of defence is to try to prevent them accessing the building in the first place. Blocking entry points in the case of rodents is essential. In the case of silverfish – always a concern in libraries, due to them eating paper – ensuring that conditions are not damp (their required habitat) will help with control. Where necessary, pest control measures will be used, a service that is frequently outsourced to specialist companies with relevant certification in the use of chemical or other agents. Co-ordination between FM and library teams on timing of visits, location of traps and other activities is important to avoid concerns on the part of library users.

Grounds maintenance

The priority for grounds maintenance outside the library is to enable safe access. This may mean treating paths so that they are not slippery, removing leaves or gritting in low temperatures where there is a risk of ice or snow. Trees need regular assessment to reduce the risk of injury to people or damage to buildings from falling branches, and care to maintain them in healthy condition. Regular litter clearing should be in place; the frequency will be assessed according to the local conditions. Once the priorities of protecting health and safety are covered, grounds maintenance can work on enhancing the external environment, e.g., with planting and seating.

Catering

Provision of food and drink falls within the remit of FM in some universities. Library management will provide information on whether food and drink are allowed in all or some of the library spaces and may work with the catering team on aspects of the provision, such as opening hours (which may increase during exam periods). The university will agree financial requirements for catering, whether to break even, make a profit or be subsidised, which will affect the decisions that can be made by the catering team.

Emergency response

FM teams may be involved alongside library staff in responding to emergency events that affect the library. A flash flood that hit the University of Plymouth demonstrates the different responsibilities that may be taken on.

Working together on flood response
Following extreme rain in the city of Plymouth on the morning of Sunday, 4 July 2021, a library information assistant found that the carpet tiles on the lowest level of the library were wet. Further inspection found that the water level increased in the north-east section and near the stairwell. A warning sign was immediately placed in the area and the security team was contacted. Security officers came to the site and undertook further inspections with the information assistant, but the root cause could not be established. Library managers came onto campus and a student ambassador was used to prevent students from accessing the lower level and to take their requests for books, which were then fetched by library staff, where possible. Heavy rain fell again, and this further affected the lower level. The library team and anyone else who was available on-site from FM worked together to move furniture, electrical appliances and other items away from the water and the fire service was called. Water continued to enter the building during the morning and the library was closed at 13:00hrs. The Head of Building and Engineering was present and assessed the risks, particularly electrical, and brought in external contractors to make a further evaluation and confirm safety.

The library team remained present throughout, helping to remove the water while maintaining continuity of service. Eventually, an industrial-size dehumidifier was brought in to dry the area.

Following the initial response, the library team identified a specialist storage facility where materials could be moved, as the space had to be emptied to enable remedial works to take place. Facilities staff assisted with packing and moving boxes. The Building and Engineering team worked with contractors to identify the underlying issue and put in place works to rectify it. They managed the works and the subsequent redecoration of the area. The flooded area was unavailable for library use for approximately three months while the building works were carried out.

Capital development: library engagement with university estates and facilities teams
Context
Like all commercial and public buildings, university libraries seek to keep pace with new trends and the changing demands of students and staff. In recent times, there has been demand for more casual group study space that provides users with less formal seating and collaborative working

environments where discussions can take place. There is an expectation that some spaces will be more akin to café-type environments that have coffee and snacks on hand, but that also have high-quality Wi-Fi, good lighting and adequate provision of power sockets for charging equipment such as laptops, tablets and other devices. This requires very careful design to ensure that the overall ambience of the building is not negatively impacting on those wanting more formal, quiet study space. Libraries are very popular spaces, and the demand for extended opening hours results in the buildings' fabric and infrastructure having to work hard, which reduces the life expectancy of the respective assets.

It is important that estates and facilities teams develop good working relationships with library management colleagues to ensure that library buildings are well operated and appropriately refurbished and upgraded to meet customer expectations. Library management teams will typically have a key person (or persons) such as a facilities manager or facilities co-ordinator who will take the lead role in ensuring that day-to-day operations allow business as usual to take place. They also liaise with estates and facilities colleagues to ensure co-ordination of any planned or reactive maintenance, thereby ensuring smooth operation of the library and that the building users' needs are satisfied. These staff will also be the key contacts for any planned refurbishment and upgrading work, to ensure that known issues are addressed and any lessons learned can be actioned.

Typically, there will be monthly meetings between key library and estates and facilities colleagues where any current issues can be raised and any planned maintenance activities can be discussed in advance of the works being undertaken. Minutes should be kept that record the information discussed, actions to be taken forward and who is tasked with those actions.

Once a project for the library has been identified, it is important to bring the various key stakeholders together to ensure that the project can be properly briefed. A typical steering group is shown in Figure 1.1 on the next page.

Capital development project process

New build, refurbishment and larger-value maintenance projects are normally executed utilising the Royal Institute of British Architects (RIBA) Plan of Work (RIBA, 2020). This plan organises the process of briefing, designing, constructing and operating building projects into eight stages and explains the stage outcomes, core tasks and information exchanges required at each stage.

* POE = Post Occupancy Evaluation
Figure 1.1 *Typical project steering group*

- Stage 0 – Strategic definition – Establishing the project objectives, initial feasibility studies and initial briefings. This should align with the university's strategy and the library's operational plan.
- Stage 1 – Preparation and briefing – Refining the project requirements, developing feasibility studies and finalising and agreeing the client project brief.
- Stage 2 – Concept design – Generating the initial design concepts to help engage with the client and thereafter obtain client approval.
- Stage 3 – Spatial co-ordination – Performing detailed spatial planning and co-ordination, often involving space consultants and specialists.
- Stage 4 – Technical design – Developing detailed technical drawings and specifications for construction that will form part of the tender documentation.
- Stage 5 – Manufacturing and construction – The actual construction phase, including site preparation, building erection and installation of services.
- Stage 6 – Handover – Completing construction, commissioning systems and handing over the building to the client, including training staff in how to operate and maintain the systems.

- Stage 7 – In Use – Undertaking post-occupancy evaluation, ongoing planned maintenance, and gathering lessons-learned feedback for future projects.

Each stage involves specific tasks, deliverables and milestones to ensure the project progresses smoothly from inception to completion.

It is good practice for universities to appoint external professional consultants who will come together as a team to work with the 'client' to produce the strategic definition for the project referred to as the client requirements or project brief. Most university estates and facilities departments have their own project managers (PMs) who will be allocated to a project and then expected to take it through the various RIBA plan stages. Many universities will also appoint external PMs in addition to the in-house PMs. In this model, the internal PM normally provides the conduit between the client, the design team and the contractor. The external PM directs the design team and the contractor for the project to be executed in line with the RIBA plan and to ensure that the project is delivered to achieve the client brief on time and within budget.

It is worth noting that the 'client' can be a range of departments across the university and the library, all of whom should be consulted and given the opportunity to contribute to the production of the project brief. This includes library management and facilities co-ordinators, estates and facilities teams including fabric and building services (hard FM) and security, cleaning (including waste management) and, where applicable, catering teams (soft FM) (see Figure 1.1).

The RIBA plan of work provides clear gateways and sustainability checkpoints. The model provides a template that, if followed, reduces project risks such as scope creep, poor communication, quality issues, cost overruns, non-compliance with legal and regulatory instruments and, ultimately, client dissatisfaction.

The design team can be procured in a variety of ways, the most common examples being:

1 The university appoints a multidisciplinary consultancy performing all the key roles of the design team, typically: architect, building services, structures/civils, quantity surveyor.
2 The university appoints a PM (or lead consultant) who forms a design team with other external consultants' disciplines and then acts as the single point of contact for the client and has full responsibility for managing the output and performance of the design team.

3 The university directly appoints individual consultants of different disciplines, with one of these being appointed as the lead consultant who fulfils the role of co-ordinating the work of the full design team but who does not necessarily have management responsibility for the design team. The lead consultant can then report to the internal PM and/or the separately appointed external PM.

4 The university appoints a contractor to provide a full turnkey project that includes the full design and construction. This involves approaching the market with a high-level strategic brief that defines the project requirements, objectives and scope. It is essential to ensure alignment with internal governance, statutory regulations, budget constraints and stakeholder needs. This step often involves creating a detailed brief or specification document.

Traditional versus design-and-build construction

The above examples allow the client to develop the project in a phased manner in alignment with the RIBA plan of works. A typical approach for delivering projects is for the design team to develop the design sufficiently to allow it to be competitively tendered. The tender is then issued to bidders and the contract is awarded to the successful bidder. The contractor then executes the works as per the design. The design team is retained by the client, the design responsibility and risks associated with it being retained by the client.

It has recently become more common for universities to novate the design team as part of the tender process, with the intention that the successful contractor assumes responsibility for design development through the construction phase, the construction activities, handover and post-completion phases. This allows the client to have the design sufficiently progressed to allow a higher degree of cost certainty based on the client's own developed and approved design. The works can then be tendered to construction contractors with the transfer of the design responsibility (novation of the design) being included in the contract. This has advantages and disadvantages for the client, some of which are highlighted in Table 1.2 opposite.

Some organisations choose to retain the original design team as a 'shadow design team' who are then responsible for ensuring that the original design intent and specification are delivered by the contractor and their appointed design team. This has the benefit of adding a layer of quality checking, but at the expense of significant additional professional fees.

Soft Landings

Government Soft Landings (GSL) was born out of an existing process called Soft Landings developed by Building Services Research and Information

Table 1.2 *Project delivery approaches: advantages and disadvantages*

Form of contract	Advantages	Disadvantages
Traditional	• The client retains control of the design team and is therefore better placed if the design has not been fully developed and/or changes need to be made. • The design team can represent the client, thus ensuring that the contractor constructs as per their design. • Flexibility is maximised to instigate change with the least financial penalty.	• The client retains responsibility for the design risk and any additional costs incurred due to design short-comings, post contract award. • The contractor may be restricted from demonstrating innovation and opportunities to improve buildability by modifying the design, proposing alternative methods of construction or using different materials and equipment, which could save both time and costs.
Design and build (novation of original design team)	• The client transfers all design risk (including design completed before the contract award) to the contractor, including anything that might delay or impact on the programme. • The design completeness and quantification of the works lie fully with the contractor, thereby streamlining communication. • Potentially greater efficiency, as innovative design can lead to more efficient construction processes, saving time and resources.	• The client relinquishes its control of the design team. • The contractor can change the design, provided that the works still comply with the works information within the tender documentation. • The quality may be reduced, due to the contractor seeking lower-cost alternative construction methods, or to use alternative materials that may affect the physical construction, or even the overall design if designers are forced to make changes. • It is possible that the contractor will seek to compensate for cost overruns in parts of the project by cutting specification (quality) levels elsewhere, which could lead to latent defects becoming apparent later on.
Design and build (new design team)	The contractor selects their own design team, rather than being obliged to work with a design team appointed by the client. This may result in less confrontation and better team working.	• The loss of the original design team may result in loss of the original designers, along with their knowledge and insight into the project. • There may be challenges in transitioning from one design team to another, potentially leading to delays or disruptions. • The new design team may not have the same level of understanding or commitment to the project.

Association (BSRIA) and the Useable Buildings Trust (UBT). The Soft Landings Framework was launched by BSRIA and UBT in 2009 and has attracted much interest and support, including from central government who launched their own version, Government Soft Landings (GSL), in 2016. Originally the focus of the guidance developed by BSRIA and UBT was an attempt to address the very significant difference observed between the predicted and actual energy use of a building. GSL goes a lot further than the original Soft Landings process, as it addresses the additional aspects of sustainability – environmental, economic and social (including functionality and effectiveness) – by setting and tracking targets.

Soft Landings is most successfully implemented when there is early engagement with all the relevant stakeholders, the desired outcome being to ensure that new buildings or infrastructure perform as intended and meet the operational needs of the end users.

The benefits of GSL (UK BIM Framework, 2019) include the following.

- Improved performance of buildings: GSL aims to improve the performance of buildings by ensuring that they meet the requirements of end users. This involves engaging stakeholders early on and throughout the project life cycle to address potential issues and optimise performance.
- Reduction in operational costs: By focusing on operational performance from the outset, GSL aims to reduce long-term operational costs associated with building maintenance, energy consumption and overall efficiency. This proactive approach can lead to savings in the long run.
- Enhanced user satisfaction: GSL emphasises understanding and meeting the needs of end users, resulting in buildings that better serve their purposes. This leads to increased satisfaction among occupants or users of the building.
- Long-term sustainability: Implementing GSL can contribute to creating more sustainable buildings by ensuring that they are efficient in their use of resources, leading to reduced environmental impact over their life cycle.
- Early issue identification: GSL encourages early identification and resolution of issues during the design and construction phases, preventing problems from carrying over to the operational stage.
- Knowledge transfer: GSL facilitates knowledge transfer between project teams, stakeholders and end users, ensuring that operational insights are shared and utilised throughout the project life cycle.
- Risk mitigation: By focusing on understanding user needs and performance requirements, GSL helps to mitigate risks associated with potential operational issues or discrepancies between design intent and practical use.

- Compliance and standards: GSL aligns with industry standards and compliance requirements, ensuring that buildings meet regulatory and performance standards from the outset.
- Continuous improvement: The approach encourages a culture of continuous improvement, enabling feedback loops and adjustments post-completion to optimise building performance over time.

Overall, GSL offers a systematic and collaborative approach to delivering buildings that not only meet the initial design specifications but also perform optimally in terms of efficiency, functionality and end user satisfaction throughout their life cycle. Consideration should be given to when the full implementation of GSL is appropriate, but the general principals can be adapted and scaled to suit projects and maintenance works that are smaller in scale, complexity and cost.

Building Information Model (BIM)

Most universities will now include a requirement for BIM level 2 to be incorporated into major project works. This requires all the design team to work collaboratively within a three-dimensional space model where all construction design is co-ordinated to ensure that fabric and services clashes can be avoided. The model also provides the opportunity for all assets to be specified, and full details are imported into the model. Manufacturers of furniture and equipment therefore prepare Computer Aided Design (CAD) drawings and specification information that can be imported into the model, including a full list of product details such as dimensions, performance information, spare parts, warranty, etc. All this information is then updated as the construction works progress, the intention being that it will be available to the client at project handover to provide the operations team responsible for maintaining the assets with easy access to all the relevant information, facilitating ease of operation and maintenance. The information can be extracted from the model in the form of a dataset called Construction Operations Building Information Exchange (COBie). This is a non-proprietary data format for the publication of a subset of BIMs, focused on delivering asset data as distinct from the geometric information. The COBie file can then be imported into proprietary maintenance Computer Aided Facilities Management (CAFM) systems to add the building assets and allow the various maintenance activities to be scheduled within the planned maintenance module. Alternatively, the data can be exported to a spreadsheet (e.g., Microsoft Excel) to produce a comprehensive asset register. The benefits of having a comprehensive asset register cannot be overstated: it is a tool to ensure that all assets are scheduled for planned maintenance as per statutory compliance, best practice and in satisfation of requirements to keep manufacturers' warranties valid. Provided the contractor has accurately populated the BIM with the asset information, the COBie file can be adapted by the FM team to integrate the data into the relevant CAFM system. This will include the manufacturer's model, serial number and date of manufacture.

Standard specification

University estates and facilities teams normally develop some standard specification documentation for building fabric, building services, equality and diversity, and hard and soft landscaping. These specifications are an attempt to ensure that tried and tested products are used and that any that have performed poorly, have a short life or prove difficult and/or expensive to replace are avoided.

The library team has a key role to play in identifying elements of the building fabric and services that work well, are easy to use and have longevity, as well as any elements that keep breaking down or do not stand up to considerable use, leading to premature failure and necessary replacement. All this feedback can be included in the standard specification documentation prepared by the estates and facilities team to produce a list of those items that are tried and tested and others that have not performed well and can be avoided.

It is essential to ensure that all items specified provide good value for money and have a long operational life, and that future maintenance, repair and eventual replacement costs have been considered from the outset. All too often, clients allow their design teams to specify items that may have higher initial costs and do not provide value for money in terms of whole-life costing. Often these items prove expensive to replace on a like-for-like basis from operational budgets that are normally under considerable pressure.

Sustainability and journey to net zero

It is an essential part of every project to consider sustainability in all aspects of the design brief and to identify opportunities to reduce energy consumption and the carbon footprint of the building. University libraries are typically open for extended hours and operate seven days per week. As such, they consume a lot of power and other resources. Careful consideration needs to be given to ensuring that designs help to reduce consumption and minimise waste. Lighting should be low-energy LED (light-emitting diode) technology, with occupancy and dimming capabilities. Building Energy Management Systems (BEMS) should be utilised to ensure that the building's heating and cooling are optimised and that plant can be set back or switched off when spaces are not occupied. Renewable heating and power technologies should also be considered and, where possible, adopted.

Again, the library FMs and co-ordinators can play a key role in helping to develop the design brief so as to ensure that known occupancy patterns and individual space requirements are fully considered and the design is as sustainable as possbile, and to help achieve a reduction in the building's carbon emissions.

Changes to FM services in response to changing library use

Libraries are changing their relationships with users and over recent years have been evolving their functions and the ways in which they operate. Pedagogical changes have led to increasing amounts of social learning spaces being needed, providing students with the choice of working in groups or booking break-out rooms and with access to more traditional book stacks. During the COVID-19 pandemic restrictions many libraries moved to a service where material could be ordered and collected, changing the relationship that some students have with the library.

These changes have an impact on the spaces that are provided by FM. New social learning spaces are being designed, and furniture that can be used in different ways and moved around by users is being sourced and included as part of larger projects, or just to enhance existing spaces.

The different uses of the library can result in changes to the FM services, e.g., group study spaces may need to be cleaned more frequently than desks, as students eat and drink while discussing, and heating and ventilation requirements may change as the building is used at different times of day. FM needs to understand the changing uses so as to enable services to vary and be provided effectively and efficiently. This understanding can come in part from monitoring usage, e.g., through occupancy sensors and from ongoing collaboration with library colleagues.

Conclusion

Libraries are at the heart of the university estate and are regarded as a key resource supporting the student experience. Typically, they operate seven days per week with extended operating times, often providing 24-hour access. As such, they place a high demand on library operational managers and estates and facilities teams to ensure that the building fabric and supporting infrastructure are well maintained and that there is a robust asset maintenance plan that will ensure that systems are replaced before the end of their operational life. Undertaking capital and maintenance works requires good communication and co-ordination between the library and estates teams to minimise the impact on users.

It is essential that changes in pedagogy and technology are reflected in the future provision of library services. Therefore, library leaders and their support teams and FM teams should meet regularly, with an established agenda that covers operational issues and development requirements. Any planned redevelopment projects or larger fabric and infrastructure replacement and upgrading works should be discussed in detail so as to agree the scope of the proposed works. This should consider what has worked well and what not so well, and adopt lessons learned while embracing the opportunity to modernise facilities with a view to future-proofing them for the short to medium term. This should include the opportunity to reduce carbon emissions and energy costs in alignment with the institution's journey towards net zero targets.

References

European Facility Management Network (EUROFM) (2024) FM Standards, https://eurofm.org/about-fm/fm-standards.

RIBA (2020) RIBA Plan of Work 2020 Overview, RIBA, www.architecture.com/knowledge-and-resources/resources-landing-page/riba-plan-of-work.

UK BIM Framework (2019) Government Soft Landings: Revised Guidance for the Public Sector on Applying BS8536 Parts 1 and 2, Updated for ISO 19650, https://ukbimframework.org/wp-content/uploads/2019/11/GSL_Report_PrintVersion.pdf.

Wiggins, J. M. (2014) *Facilities Manager's Desk Reference, 2nd Edition*, Wiley Blackwell.

2

Academic Libraries and Estates Strategy: A Library Leadership Perspective

Tim Wales

Introduction

In my 20 years' professional experience of leading five UK academic or research libraries, *the* most difficult, frustrating yet essential institutional relationship has been with the estates or facilities department. Throughout this chapter, 'estates department' or 'estates director' refers to the people and senior leader who manage, maintain and develop the physical infrastructure of a university and its associated services and utilities. The latter services can include the management of catering facilities, vending machines and student accommodation – which I define as 'facilities' even though 'estates' and 'facilities' are often used interchangeably. The importance of the estates/library services relationship has intensified in line with the increased higher education (HE) sector focus on 'student experience' during the 2000s as evidenced in the United Kingdom's (UK) National Student Survey (NSS), a national tool for benchmarking student satisfaction, as well as with the marketisation of HE in the UK.

Unlike other HE support services which can (rightly or wrongly) be replicated in some part at department level to enable local control and oversight of specialist or niche library functions, e.g., the library systems team, the security/reception team, porters, etc., the same is not true of estates services and their unique remit to maintain and develop the institutional estate. Yes, it is true that most large libraries employ some form of facilities or environment manager post, but such a role is mainly concerned with managing relationships and service levels on behalf of the head of service with estates colleagues and their sub-contractors. Such a role is rarely involved in the nuts and bolts of planning or constructing a new building or directly responsible for maintaining an existing library estate. This fact, in my view, creates a form of perpetual insecurity and paranoia arising from the lack of control over a key part of library operations that shades the working relationship between library and estates teams, especially when the library team are fielding estates-related calls from their customers.

I have no doubt too that some library services are perceived as tricky and awkward internal customers by our estates colleagues – never happy with their lot, impatient, always complaining, not understanding the reality of balancing competing demands on a limited resource across a complex estate with many legal obligations to remember, etc. So often in my experience, though, at the heart of this mismatch is the fact that the budget and planning cycles of both sides seem to be out of sync so that the demands of one side cannot be met by the other due to the point in the financial cycle. Sometimes only an intervention by the university executive promising additional funds or a reprioritisation of the estates plan seems to be able to restore the equilibrium.

As a final introductory note, I am conscious of the fact that I have not yet seen a new library estates project through from idea to completion *in one institution*. However, on reflection, I realise that I have participated in most of the different Royal Institute of British Architects (RIBA) stages associated with such projects when my career is viewed in totality across multiple institutions (RIBA, 2020). This pattern does perhaps reflect the reality for most UK academic library heads who have had to change jobs and progress upwards in seniority via several institutions to reach a leadership position. In doing so, they may have missed the rare career opportunity to be involved in creating a new library building from scratch, usually inheriting an existing project part-way through.

Survey

As the above very much represents my own experience gained from working at various academic or research institutions, for the benefit of this book I decided to survey my fellow UK academic library heads in November 2023 on their experiences of working with their estates departments.

I used the private SCONUL-DIRS JISC mailing list as my sampling frame for a Qualtrics online survey, as the Society of College, National and University Libraries (SCONUL) is the main UK and Ireland professional membership organisation for academic and research libraries (SCONUL, 2024). The list had 218 individual members (excluding SCONUL staff) representing 190 member institutions at the time of the survey. Fifty-four responses were received representing 28% of SCONUL member institutions. Respondents were asked to indicate which UK HE mission group their institution belonged to, as I believed this to be a short cut for understanding respective higher education institution (HEI) size, type (research-intensive or teaching-intensive) and mission in the context of library provision (Table 3.1). The average number of student FTEs serviced by respondents (n=51) was 20,303 from either 1 site library (31%) or 2–5 site libraries (61%), with only 8% running 6 or more site libraries.

I believe this to be the first survey on this library topic attempted and codified in the UK since 2000, and so there was no previous questionnaire to draw from in the literature. This means that some of the survey questions did have a detectable bias which at least one respondent picked up on in their free text comments. Nevertheless, I will try to weave in the findings from the rich survey results as appropriate as the chapter unfolds.

Whose space is it anyway and what are the drivers for decisions on spaces?

To what extent are library heads the masters of their own (physical) universe? Are they able to make the ultimate decisions on new library spaces or major refurbishments, when all is said and done? In my experience this depends on the institutional culture, the power dynamics at play within it and the various drivers prevalent in the period in question, as the following case studies from personal experience will illustrate.

Case study 1: The Paul Hamlyn Library at the University of West London (UWL)

This is an excellent example of an integrated estates redevelopment and master plan with a new library literally at its heart. The library adjoins an atrium called 'The Heartspace', which was created by demolishing old teaching blocks at the centre of the main campus. The vice chancellor was the driving force behind most major UWL change projects and Library Services was helped by the fact that he was generally pro libraries and had preconceptions of what an ideal library should be (including the optimum size of a printed book collection for academic credibility).

Investment in a new library was also one of many firm commitments the vice chancellor made to address legacy poor NSS satisfaction scores, alongside the creation of a new Student Experience portfolio for an incoming pro-vice chancellor who would be able to bring much-needed co-ordination to student experience services and projects, something that had become intrinsically bound up with the ongoing major estates renovation project (for example, should there be a shared reception and office area for Student Services staff as a prominent focal point for students, while optimising space use).

From an incoming head of library point of view, I was expected to lead the completion of the development of the new library with the director of estates. We had to make the most of the empty box, which was already under construction before I joined UWL, that was to become the new library, deciding how best to use the space for collections and services and accompanying designs.

Although part of the University's senior management team, I was probably third or fourth in the institutional 'pecking order' for library estates decisions, but we were all working to the same goal within a relatively short time frame (12–18 months), which was to relocate the main library back to the campus from a temporary location in an office block one mile away and offer students a modern library building suitable for different study styles and collections. After an uncertain start working with the architect's original floor layouts, a very productive working relationship developed once I had persuaded the director of estates to employ a specialist library design consultancy alongside the architects. The consultancy was able to bring a new injection of ideas and enthusiasm into our design thinking, underpinned with excellent attention to detail (especially when determining the optimum balance of collections versus study spaces, considering floor-loading factors, etc.). They were able to offer visualisations based on their experiences of the HE sector and working within a limited budget and, crucially from my perspective, were able to resource a much-needed (and rapid) in-person student consultation survey before the summer vacation to provide an extra sanity check on some of our fit-out ideas. The report on the survey's key findings, as it was student focused and presented directly to the project board by the consultants, enabled me to rise up that pecking order, and on the back of it I was able to successfully make the case for some additional investment in radio frequency identification (RFID) technology, new book stock and various design changes before it was too late.

The new library building opened in summer 2015 and was very well received by the student body, to the point that it was instrumental in library services' NSS scores ultimately reaching 90+% in subsequent years, rising from the mid-70s a few years earlier. Not everything was rosy with the estates team, however; the director of estates ultimately expressed disappointment in how the entrance area of the new library manifested itself in the end, 'lacking a wow factor' to lure students inside.

Case study 2: The Likiermann Library in the Sammy Ofer Centre at London Business School (LBS)

This was a fascinating example of an institution taking tactical advantage of a rare opportunity to acquire the lease of a large but poorly maintained council-owned facility (the Old Marylebone Town Hall (OMTH)) to meet LBS's long-standing strategic aim of expanding its teaching footprint in a very expensive and built-up part of London. A substantial £25 million donation to LBS funded the refurbishment and remodelling of the building (LBS, 2017).

As a head of library reporting to the director of IT, who reported to the chief operating officer (COO), I was not privy to many of the senior machinations behind the project, unlike at UWL in the previous case study. This comparative lack of seniority was the outcome of a major restructuring exercise to reduce support staff costs after a downturn in the executive MBA market during the 2010 recession. The director of information services role was deleted, and the library team was halved in size and moved into IT services. This was quite a change in status, as compared to the 1970s when the LBS librarian was a board member. Unlike UWL, the driving force in delivering the project was not the dean but the University secretary (rather than the COO or estates department), as they were already involved in the complex legal and planning negotiations and truly represented both the spirit of the School and the School's best interests.

As the project planning progressed, it became apparent that there were discussions as to whether the LBS library should be relocated into OMTH from its existing location opposite the main campus building. From a head of library perspective, this presented a once-in-a-decade opportunity to gain some rare capital investment in library space and facilities as part of a flagship building project. However, it also presented a potential risk in terms of declining student footfall, as OMTH was further away from the main campus.

From an estates team point of view, moving the library would release additional space at its existing location for a much-requested gym extension and additional executive development teaching space without having to construct additional buildings. Even more importantly, it transpired that the local planning department would look favourably upon any redevelopment plans that preserved the original layouts and library use of the OMTH Annex (Grade II listed) with its rotunda reading room, original book lift and other wooden fittings. It was this planning permission incentive that finally made the argument for the LBS library to relocate, despite the operational challenges that this would ultimately create.

I did not stay long enough at LBS to see the project through to completion, so it is for my successors to judge whether or not the move was a success for the service in terms of, e.g., institutional visibility and student footfall. As with the earlier UWL case study, I am aware that the LBS library was able to successfully use the move to upgrade its self-check and security hardware to use RFID technology. And the restored rotunda reading room is a lovely space. However, the extent to which the head of library could have insisted on any other option for the library is very unclear, given their position and status in the organisational structure as described earlier.

Case study 3: Rothamsted Research Library

Rothamsted Research (RRes) is an independent UK agricultural research institution with a long, complex and illustrious history (Rothamsted Research, 2024). In the mid-2010s, the actual power to get things done there estates-wise lay with both the 'Station Engineer' (as the director of estates was then known) and the chief financial officer (CFO), even though the head of library and information services reported directly to the chief executive officer (CEO).

The CEO was keen on the idea of reconfiguring the existing relatively small but underused RRes library space to create more internal meeting rooms that would be free for institutional use (whereas use of rooms in the adjoining conference centre had to be paid for via internal budgets as part of a new funding deal put in place with the Biotechnology and Biological Sciences Research Council (BBSRC), Lawes Agricultural Trust and Rothamsted Enterprises Ltd). Inevitably, RRes staff went to great lengths to avoid using the paid-for spaces, which put a premium on the few remaining spaces dotted around the campus, many of which were poorly fitted out for teleconferencing.

In two minds about the plan, as I knew it would increase footfall while potentially creating some conflicting space use, I drew up some sample layouts with the Station Engineer, who was fatalistic about the probability of anything actually happening as a result. Sure enough the then CFO was able to block any such library space works on priority and cost grounds, despite the initial enthusiasm of the CEO. The library therefore remained as is, and will do so until the space it currently occupies can be converted into commercial laboratory space to be let out by Rothamsted Enterprises Ltd. The moral of this case study is that sometimes even having the support of the CEO or vice chancellor is not enough for heads of libraries to force through library space projects with the estates department, due to the power dynamics (or financial realities) at play in institutions.

Survey analysis

Findings from my survey for this chapter are perhaps even more illuminating when considered alongside the case studies above. Table 2.2 shows the responses to the question which aimed to identify which senior officer really did have the final say (according to the respondents, at least) over library building and spaces at the respondents' institutions. The phrasing of the question perhaps indicated that I was not expecting the answer to be the head of library service – and the results showed that this was indeed the case!

That role ended up being third most-cited from the list of choices presented (17% of responses) with first and second in importance being the COO (29%) and vice chancellor (25%), respectively. Of course, institutional governance structures and hierarchies vary, but nevertheless it is salutary to note that effectively 83% of respondents indicated that the head of library services was not ultimately responsible for their own library building(s)! It was ever thus – prestigious libraries such as the Bodleian at Oxford were conceived and shaped by wealthy and ambitious alumni such as Thomas

Bodley, rather than by the scholar librarians who ran them (Pettegree and der Weduwen, 2022).

'Bargaining chips' for library–estates negotiations

It is very rare, in my experience, for library heads to be permanent members of estates strategy committees in UK universities. The estates director is usually the more senior of the two positions in terms of responsibility, budget and position in corporate governance (e.g., reporting directly to the vice chancellor or COO) and so the library head inevitably becomes a supplicant as my earlier case studies showed.

So what other leverage does the library head have over the estates department in negotiations to get library needs prioritised? These are discussed in more detail elsewhere in this book, but, in my experience, examples can include the following.

- **Student experience:** For students, the site library is usually the main third space (i.e., that used most after home and work/education spaces) on campus. It is usually the space open for the longest and so it gets the most throughput and student attention. If a UK academic library service's NSS score is particularly low as compared to the sector average – and the free text comments indicate that this is mainly due to the state of the physical environment – then the senior executive team usually notices and puts pressure on the head of estates.
- **Prestige or reputational factors:** An unsightly physical library environment can get attention when it is noticed at institutional open days, public events or student union activity. Sometimes bringing attention to this situation during a formal committee with the vice chancellor present can provoke a response.
- **Planning related:** Examples include listed building status or planning gain from resurrecting library activity (see Case study 2).
- **Space savings:** Examples include co-location of services or compression of space to achieve better space use efficiencies so as to save money elsewhere on campus (but once released, unlikely to be regained). This is often wrapped up in bigger conversations around site sales or campus consolidation efforts.
- **Environmental costs:** If the building is too costly to heat or maintain, then this should force the estates team's hand – depending on how bad are the conditions of other buildings!
- **Compliance or standards requirements:** For example, the need to meet the Society of Legal Scholars' requirements for law collections as part of a bid for accreditation (Society of Legal Scholars, 2009).

- **Cost savings:** These could come from reductions in leasing spaces from third parties, or from a more energy-efficient space, or from using a space-accounting method based on equivalent commercial rent charge per square metre.
- **External stakeholder factors:** These can include benefactors, council member interest, funding grants, and so on.
- **Competition and prestige factors:** These are typically applicable to regional or historic rivalries between research-intensive institutions such as Cambridge, Oxford and University College London.

Of course, any combination of the above can apply, but often the same combination becomes less effective over time as each party understands more about how the other tends to operate and they learn to work together. Ultimately, the library service is not purely looking to negotiate, to fight for or to protect its own position, but to produce the best outcome for the institution, which can only be done by negotiating with other stakeholders.

Survey findings

I wanted to test my list of 'bargaining chips' against the experience of my peers in the academic library sector, so I asked my survey respondents to rank a list of negotiating tactics or arguments used with estates departments to 'get things' done in order of effectiveness. The results are shown here in rank order (1 = highest voted, $n = 48$):

1 development of good personal relationships in advance
2 student experience
3 compliance with regulations, professional standards, health and safety, etc.
4 green or environmental considerations
5 cost savings
6 space savings
7 reduction in complaints
8 prestige or reputational factors for the institution
9 use of senior management views to exert pressure
10 benchmarking/peer-group comparisons
11 library or archival collection concerns.

The top three are broadly in line with my personal experience and it is tempting to cluster items 4–6 together under an overall efficiency banner, with one eye on the current economic climate in the UK, which is still recovering, in gross domestic product terms, from the COVID-19 pandemic.

But perhaps the most striking conclusion from these results, especially to our illustrious librarian forebears, is of how little importance the core aspects of librarianship relating to collection management and stewardship are in this list. Is this because the post-World War 2 expansion in UK university library buildings solved those space constraints long ago? Or is it because of the focus since 2000 on study and learning spaces – rather than space for collections – to meet the rapid rise in undergraduate numbers across the UK HE sector after various government reforms? Further research is needed.

Finally, not a 'bargaining chip' per se, but a definite means of facilitating the library–estates relationship is the employment of a dedicated or semi-dedicated estates liaison post in the library management team. It is most often deployed on a fixed-term basis during major library estates projects, whether new-builds, extensions or refurbishments, but some larger library services (in terms of either physical estate or student numbers) deploy a facilities manager role all year round. The role is attractive from a head of library perspective, as recruitment is usually not dependent on library qualifications (or, indeed, facilities management qualifications). It is also an attractive secondment or redeployment opportunity for existing staff. It enables the burden of day-to-day estates communications and troubleshooting to be shared, and ensures that there is some dedicated staff resource available to be spent on project planning, supplier liaison, external scanning, etc. From an estates department point of view, it reduces the complexity of business, partnering with one dedicated point of contact, and enables them to habituate or train the post holder in their preferred way of working and culture before translating that back to the library stakeholder groups.

Library, IT and estates relationships

One aspect that I was not able to cover in the survey was the extent to which IT considerations also influence thinking around estates and library projects nowadays. Developments in, and student expectations around, universal Wi-Fi access and device portability are obviating the need to provide traditional IT teaching labs laid out in linear rows, or hundreds of fixed personal computers in new-builds. Virtual server hosting (whether on a local campus cloud or in a private cloud) is reducing the number of server rooms needed to support connectivity in campus spaces. As students can now roam and gather flexibly to study as they like without being tethered to physical devices (with the possible exception of power sockets until wireless charging becomes prevalent), so flexibility in space and infrastructure design is needed to attract them to study on campus. Otherwise, they will vote with their feet and base themselves on the nearest coffee chain's sofas.

The fast pace of technological change means that the types of physical IT hardware and infrastructure needing to be considered by library leaders when thinking about new or refurbished library estates in 2024 include the following.

- **Library RFID technology:** This includes self-service kiosks, reservation/laptop lockers, sensor alarms and sorting systems (for medium- to large-circulation libraries). Kiosks may disappear during the next decade, once self-checkout and return via mobile becomes prevalent or libraries truly become e-only, but considerations of the library 'security perimeter' can still dominate estates thinking, such as at UWL (see Wales, 2017).
- **Audio-visual (AV) display technologies:** Whether in classrooms, study pods or circulation areas (digital signage), with wireless connectivity these have become less bulky, although they do require more associated furniture for facilitating hybrid meetings. Virtual reality headsets and 3D immersive spaces are also starting to appear.
- **Personal computing hardware:** Increasingly, dual monitors with docking stations for laptops are provided. Some library software still requires desktop architecture, so a 100% move to tablet devices is not expected until the 2030s.
- **Swipe-control access systems:** These allow flexible provisioning of different areas according to user types (although it is still amazing how widespread physical locks and keys remain across UK library estates).
- **Scanning and printing multifunctional devices (MFDs):** These take up less space than pure photocopiers in the past (including paper storage space). Some libraries have gone down the maker-space route as well, of course, with provision of 3D printer spaces, but no UK academic libraries to date have gone down the 'print on demand' equipment and supply route typified by the now defunct Espresso Book Machine.
- **Security surveillance systems:** These comprise remote-controlled cameras in key hotspots linked to intelligent surveillance systems across the wider university estate, with people-tracking abilities.

The extent to which the institutional IT strategy shapes or is shaped by the above is a question worthy of discussion elsewhere.

Future trends in academic library builds from a leadership perspective

Other than changes in materials, emphasis and interior design trends, it is hard to identify any major new trends in UK academic library design in this century. The oft-discussed possibility of moving to a true e-only library from a collections point of view has yet to materialise, not least due to the current controversy and uncertainty around e-book pricing models (Anderson, 2023). The cost to an average-sized UK HE institution of replacing a standard library's print textbook teaching collection with equivalent e-textbook accesses for the required number of students would run into the high tens of millions of pounds alone, by my estimates, before even considering the additional costs of moving to e-monographs (presuming that they would all be available in online form across the disciplines needed). Even when digitising archive or special collections, the primary source materials and artefacts usually need to be retained somewhere. Print collections are therefore here to stay and must be factored into library estates planning even if they are reduced in size and relocated to less-prime real estate either on or off campus.

Unfortunately, the collaborative collection storage schemes (whether regional or national) needed to release the space to achieve this aim have yet to appear in the UK. This is despite the relative success of the UK Research Reserve (UKRR) scheme for journals in the 2010s (see Stubbs and Banks, 2020) and is perhaps attributable to the slow progress on the UK National Monograph Strategy project (Showers, 2014). Nevertheless, I outline below two potential future avenues of exploration which I believe library leaders can own, rather than wait for other ideas to come to fruition or be imposed on them by directors of estates.

The warehouse model
In theory
An Amazon, Ocado or British Library automated warehouse model combined with a post-COVID-19 'click and collect' service delivery ethos offers a different library design option for UK universities in areas such as London where estates are already crammed with buildings and land value is high. I had active discussions around this concept with the executive director of estates at Brunel University London, for example, in 2021, when we were considering how best to relaunch a less ambitious version of a c. £100 million campus redevelopment project that had been postponed after the site-clearance stage due to the COVID-19 pandemic.

The theory was sound: build a comparatively low-cost, high-density storage unit on the edge of campus for a reduced-size library 'reserve' collection, with a smaller open-access teaching or textbook collection retained in the main student-facing building, releasing more floor space for it to be a multipurpose teaching and study environment with a market-place of student services on the ground floor, including a library collection point for hourly book deliveries from the store. The store didn't have to have automated book-handling conveyor systems like the British Library, but could adopt radical 'chaotic' book storage principles (i.e., that do not rely on shelving items in traditional library class-mark order) and intelligent pick software to reduce the pick-and-return delays created by having to retain shelving classification sequences in the store (see, e.g., Lyngsoe Systems, 2024). Optionally, the store could have a climate-controlled and fire-resistant facility for records and archives, which would be cheaper to create from scratch than trying to insert it retrospectively into a 1970s shell. Although, in theory, this storage model could be outsourced to a commercial off-site storage provider specialising in documents, in practice it was felt that being able to offer a possible 'within the hour' fetch system on-site was highly desirable. In addition, effectively moving library storage costs from a capital to an operational budget at a time of reducing student numbers was not desirable or feasible.

In practice
The actual delivery of fetched items to the customer would be at a small collection point in the atrium area of the refurbished building which could be used flexibly with other professional service functions, removing the need for library-specific areas with library-specific equipment such as self-checkout and return kiosks. Indeed, the current trend for self-service reserved-item collection lockers is a natural fit with the collection-point principle and removes the need for a permanent staff presence.

On closer examination, however, this 'warehouse model' is the old-fashioned closed-access library model or reference library model still found in national libraries today. The question for library and estates teams is whether the potential economies of scale from space maximisation, etc. outweigh the intangible pedagogical benefits for students of being able to browse and scan books on shelves themselves, organised by traditional classification schemes in discipline clusters. Perhaps the need for that is less now that students can browse and skim e-book versions online, especially in STEM subjects; it is predominantly for arts and humanities subjects that the traditional arrangement still has benefits. Or maybe the warehouse model is best applied retrospectively in urban campuses where space is at a premium, whereas a new-build project can still benefit from the best of both worlds.

Artificial intelligence (AI)/robotics applications
At a networking lunch with my colleague who heads up Cranfield University's facilities department (which manages most 'front of house' estates services such as catering, hotel, security, mail and residential services),

he mentioned that he was genuinely interested in the potential of robotics to reduce his staffing costs, having attended a conference with presentations from Japan, where, of course, robotic receptionists have been commonplace for some years. He revealed that he was also thinking seriously about how robots could reduce cleaning and room-servicing costs in the on-site conference hotel in future. This conversation got me thinking about the equivalent use cases in the academic library sector and their feasibility and desirability.

One immediate application would be the use of autonomous delivery vehicles for transporting books between site libraries and/or mail rooms. The Cranfield University campus is highly suited for testing this, due to its existing grid layout and self-contained nature away from busy urban areas, and, indeed, has been involved in autonomous vehicle research for some time already, especially for urban transit systems. Library and facilities staff already move books with reservations between our main Kings Norton library and our School of Management library about 400 m away. So, it was with that in mind that I volunteered our services to participate in a future Cranfield project in 2024 with robot manufacturer Peyk (Cranfield University, 2024a and 2024b). The ability to transport books autonomously (whether by drone or by vehicle) the 68 miles between Cranfield, Bedfordshire and our site library on the Defence Academy of the United Kingdom's campus at Shrivenham would be even more useful, but serious security concerns would need to be addressed first from a Ministry of Defence perspective. Both sites do have the advantages of having helipads or airfields, however.

Libraries are no stranger to automation, of course, and were in the vanguard of early computerisation in the service sector from the 1970s, continuing through to electromagnetic or RFID tag-based self-service and sorting technologies in the late 1990s and early 2000s, not to mention the large-scale automated handling facilities installed in the British Library for efficient mass book storage and retrieval. It is not, therefore, too much of a leap of faith to conceive of a library 'robot receptionist' using current library chat and FAQ (frequently asked questions) software as a knowledge base alongside an Alexa-like voice interface for end-user interaction.

Indeed, I had personally conceived of and prototyped a similar concept (called HOLLI for HOLographic LIbrarian) for out-of-hours library enquiries with a third-party digital signage company while at LBS Library in 2013. This used the same projection technology as was then deployed at UK airports' security control to encourage passengers to put their liquids and gels in small plastic bags, combined with a touchscreen and presence sensor. The technology proved slightly too clunky and annoying to be of practical use in the long term, but I am sure that a decade hence that may no longer be the case.

The future implications of such an idea for library and estate strategies would be to have a unified reception system across campus, with no need for a manned presence and no need to allocate space for reception desks and waiting areas. Visitors could be guided to where they needed to go with a slightly more sophisticated version of current campus or library apps with 3D 'Google-like' maps for specific directions inside buildings. Other potential deployment of robots by estates departments could follow, e.g., 24/7 internal and external cleaning devices or security K9 robot 'dogs'.

Conclusion

The future looks bright and interesting for universities when considering the examples in the previous section and the scope for collaboration and partnership that they offer to library and estate heads; a partnership already built on strong foundations, according to my survey's question on the quality of library respondents' relationships with their estates department: 73% ($n = 38$) considered it to be good or excellent with only 10% ($n = 5$) rating it as poor.

However, there is one finding from the survey that is worth retaining, as it epitomises the ongoing frustrations for library heads. Respondents ($n = 48$) were asked to indicate the extent to which they agreed with the following statements:

1 The University's Estates Strategy/Master Plan recognises the importance of library space to the institution.
2 I felt that I was able to contribute adequately to the development or updating of the University's Estates Strategy/Master Plan from a library perspective.
3 The University's executive team understands the future space needs and characteristics of the library service.
4 The University's estates team understands the future space needs and characteristics of the library service.

Although 66% either strongly agreed or somewhat agreed with statement 1 and 58% with statements 3 and 4, statement 2 scored only 39%, which means that we have a significant amount of lobbying to do as a profession to ensure that we secure the investment needed to maintain our library estate and that we are 'in the room' where such decisions are made. These two free-text survey comments perhaps best sum up the challenge and identify developing good working relationships as part of the solution.

Being heard as an expert in library spaces is particularly difficult. I feel like everyone (senior members of staff and estates team) have a view about what the library space is for and how it should change, because it is the one part of the service they can see and physically interact with. This view is often louder than ours. We have to work really hard on relationships because of this and still find ourselves in frustrating arguments sometimes. We don't experience the same challenge when it comes to other parts of our service (e.g., customer service, learning and teaching support, research services) where we are mostly recognised as collaborative professional experts.

I have found that Estates are not really the issue, it is more about getting the Library on the agenda of senior decision makers so they set priorities – Estates will then just take these forward as told to. Developing good working relations at an operational level is essential and very valuable alongside this. We are fortunate that a positive refurbishment is one that stakeholders all have an interest in maintaining, and we work from there. But it can be a challenge to keep this going when there are other, and quite often perfectly valid, Estates areas of concern across campus.

Tables

Table 2.1 *SCONUL Directors Survey: number of responses by UK mission group*

Please indicate your university's mission group	%	n
Non-aligned	44.44	24
Russell Group	20.4	11
GuildHE	9.25	5
MillionPlus	9.25	5
University Alliance	9.25	5
Cathedrals Group	7.41	4
TOTAL	100	54

Table 2.2 *SCONUL Directors Survey: responses to 'At the end of the day, who in reality has final say over matters relating to library building(s) and space(s) at your institution?'*

At the end of the day, who in reality has final say over matters relating to library building(s) and space(s) at your institution?	%	n
Chief Operating Officer	29	14
Vice Chancellor	25	12
Head of Library Service	17	8
Head of Estates Department	10	5
Other	10	5
Chief Financial Officer	4	2
Other Senior Executive team member	4	2

References

Anderson, J. (2023) Campaign to Investigate the Library Ebook Market,
https://academicebookinvestigation.org/about.

Cranfield University (2024a) Autonomous Vehicles and Intelligent Mobility,
www.cranfield.ac.uk/centres/advanced-vehicle-engineering-
centre/autonomous-vehicles-and-intelligent-mobility.

Cranfield University (2024b) UK First for Cranfield University and Peyk with
Launch of Campus Delivery Robots,
www.cranfield.ac.uk/press/news-2024/uk-first-for-cranfield-university-and-
peyk-with-launch-of-campus-delivery-robots.

LBS (2017) LBS's Sammy Ofer Centre Opens its Doors to the World,
www.london.edu/news/lbss-sammy-ofer-centre-opens-its-doors-to-the-
world-1322.

Lyngsoe Systems (2024) Intelligent Material Management System™,
https://lyngsoesystems.com/library/intelligent-material-management-
system.

Pettegree, A. and der Weduwen, A. (2022) *The Library: A Fragile History*,
Profile Books.

RIBA (2020) RIBA Plan of Work, www.architecture.com/knowledge-and-
resources/resources-landing-page/riba-plan-of-work.

Rothamsted Research (2024) The History of Rothamsted Research,
www.rothamsted.ac.uk/history-rothamsted-research.

SCONUL (2024) About SCONUL, www.sconul.ac.uk/about-us/about-sconul.

Showers, B. (2014) A National Monograph Strategy Roadmap, JISC,
www.jisc.ac.uk/sites/default/files/a-national-monograph-strategy-
roadmap.pdf.

Society of Legal Scholars (2009) Statement of Standards for University
Library Provision,
www.legalscholars.ac.uk/wp-content/uploads/2016/05/SLS-Library-for-a-
Modern-Law-School-Statement-2009.pdf.

Stubbs, T. and Banks, C. (2020) UKRR: A Collaborative Collection
Management Success Story, *UKSG Insights*, **33** (10), 1–9,
https://insights.uksg.org/articles/10.1629/uksg.503.

Wales, T. (2017) Paul Hamlyn Library: An Integral Part of UWL Campus,
CILIP Update, February, 42–3.

3

The University Library as Estates Asset: Tools for Negotiating Space in an Evolving Strategy

Regina Everitt

Introduction

University estates strategy takes a long-term view of an institution's mission, size and shape. The library, as an estate asset, generally evolves with the wider institutional strategy unless it is funded by an endowment which enables it to be discrete. Balancing the needs of current and future stakeholders is a delicate dance, as current users will want to see some benefit from enduring disruptions such as noise or displacement. Building flexibility into the design to enable spaces to expand or contract over time is an obvious solution, although this is easier said than done. But once we have built it, whether a new-build or a refurbishment, we need to continually check with the 'sitting' stakeholders to ensure that the spaces are fit for the current purpose while keeping an eye on the future. *Continually* is the operative word here, as stakeholders, space needs and institutional strategy change over time.

As the Director of the University of East London (UEL) Library, Archives and Learning Services (LALS), I have responsibility for service delivery within two modern buildings located on two out of the three UEL campus sites in East London. My team and I work with the estates projects team for any refurbishments or new buildings and the facilities management team for day-to-day operations, maintenance and security. Although the estates teams know how the library buildings are erected and maintained, my team and I know how the spaces within are used, which does not always mirror the intent of the design or programme of works. Prior to joining UEL, I worked at other London institutions where I had similar building responsibilities and worked with architects, designers, construction engineers, project managers, estates and facilities staff and cross-institutional stakeholders, including students and staff, to design, build and deliver spaces. One of my favourite past roles involved working on tenders for access-control systems, managed printing services, outsourced facilities services and general contract management.

In a previous role, I developed an early iteration of a social learning space during the time when many academic libraries were shedding their conservatively formal image in favour of more relaxed, informal spaces where students were empowered to work how and when they wanted. This included eating, drinking, talking on mobile phones, lounging on comfy furniture, moving furniture around to accommodate solo or group working – all activities that were certainly unconscionable when I was at university. Bookstores that allowed customers to browse and have a read while enjoying a coffee, even if they never made a book purchase, as well as the service models in technology retail shops influenced my thinking about service models for learning spaces that I developed and managed, as they empowered users to explore and learn at their own pace. However, just as my preferences about study spaces changed over time while I was at university and my needs evolved from undergraduate to postgraduate levels, I understand as a service leader that one size does not fit all library stakeholders. As discussed in other chapters in this book, the needs of stakeholders and, thus, the demand for space, have changed significantly over the years.

In this chapter I will explore some approaches that library leaders can take to assess space use and suitability. The estates project team may undertake a post-occupancy evaluation (POE), particularly for new builds. POE, according to the Royal Institute of British Architects (RIBA), is 'the process of obtaining feedback on a building's performance in use after it has been built and occupied' (RIBA, 2020). In its 2020 document on POE, RIBA advocated for all building projects using 'public money' to undertake a POE (RIBA, 2020). However, the library team will want a deeper understanding of how the spaces are used and experienced by users. After all, the library team, with support from the facilities team, will provide first-line support for any issues that arise during business as usual, while the estates project team will move on to the next new-build or programme of works.

I will also reflect on how my team and I navigated the unplanned addition of classrooms to the library at our main campus in Stratford. The case study will discuss the institutional drivers for the change, stakeholder relationship management and how cost, scope and time – the project management triangle – impacted on the final design (Rudder and Main, 2023).

In use or a waste of space?
With the shift to hybrid working post COVID-19, you may have noticed people with tablets or clipboards peering into offices and counting workspaces within your institution. These may have been members of the estates team assessing who is occupying the spaces, and with what frequency,

to determine space utilisation (Table 3.1 for examples). They use this data to inform decisions about how much space is needed to accommodate university business requirements.

Table 3.1 *Definitions of some space utilisation terms* (Moreland, 2014) *with author examples*

Term	Definition	Example
Occupancy	How much of the space is used, compared to capacity	100 seats are available but only 70 are used. Occupancy is 70%.
Frequency	The amount of time the space is used, compared to its availability	The space is available for 8 hours a day, 7 days a week, so 56 hours per week. However, it is being used for 6 hours a day, 5 days a week, so 30/56 hours per week. Frequency is 54%.
Utilisation	The occupancy multiplied by the frequency	Using the above examples, 70 x 56 = 3920/5600 = 70%

Library teams can take a similar approach.

Occupancy: Generally, we judge our capacity around the number of study places or seats that are available within our spaces. Our gate counters will give us metrics about footfall. If we use occupancy software, the analytics from that tool will tell us how much space is occupied. We can also carry out manual head counts. And, of course, by observing space use we can get a sense of whether we are approaching capacity. With the increase in hybrid working and course delivery, many institutions have experienced reductions in footfall. At my institution, footfall in the libraries dropped by over 50% in 2021/22 as compared to pre-COVID-19 2018/19 (UEL LALS, 2023). Although footfall is returning to pre-COVID-19 levels, at the time of writing, students are using the spaces differently. For example, post pandemic restrictions, students have been sitting in groups and watching online lectures around a single computer or laptop. Additionally, face-to-face enquiries have given way to online chat, even when students are sitting in staffed libraries.

Frequency: We know that this will ebb and flow with course timetables and other campus activities. For example, Mondays, Tuesdays and Thursdays are traditionally very busy days at all UEL campuses and Wednesday afternoons tend to be less busy so that students can take part in extracurricular activities. Fridays tend to be quieter teaching days; and evenings, Saturdays, and sometimes Sundays, will have some scheduled teaching or events. As UEL libraries are open 24/7 during most of the teaching year and exam periods, the libraries will always have some level of activity, whether teaching or other events. And when the campus is less busy with students, for example around late August, the libraries will be quieter than during the winter and spring terms.

Utilisation: The shift in activity in August, as described above, will be of interest to both the library leader and the estates team, as the underused capacity in our example above, 30% could be financially viable, such as in space rental to local communities or summer camps. However, before becoming giddy with the prospect of income generation, both the library leader and the estates team will need to consider wider university operations. Will postgraduate students be adversely impacted? Are there building or refurbishment projects happening within the library or around the university that require swing space for people, furniture or other storage? Is work required for the library space itself in preparation for a new academic year? If the space is to be hired out, what resources will be required by the users, e.g., access, equipment, security and other staffing? And let's not forget that even the library teams will need to take leave to rejuvenate before the start of the new academic year.

In short, whether the space is in use or wasted is contextual. Numbers alone cannot tell the story of what is or should be happening within a space. The team responsible for daily operations of the space must be included in any discussions about proposed changes.

A few more considerations

Once a new building or space has been built and utilisation is at the level you would expect during peak periods, does this mean that you have nailed the user experience? You may need to consider what other drivers may be impacting on space use. For example, are there other spaces on the campus where students could go if they had a choice, or are they using the new space by default? Are unexpected activities taking place in the space causing conflict or requiring intervention? An example could be students creating individual study space by enclosing themselves with mobile whiteboards and other furniture, much to the chagrin of other students and staff. Or large groups of pizza-eating undergraduates routinely congregating in a space creating a nuisance for other students.

You will also want to know who is *not* using the space. For example, are postgraduate students avoiding using the space and demanding dedicated space or a senior common room? Admittedly, some students may never need to enter a library building, as they can get the information that they need using online resources. However, you will want to know whether those for whom the space was designed are *not* using it, and why.

User experience research

User experience (UX) research enables us to understand user attitudes about and behaviour within spaces. The two differ, as we often say one thing and do another. For example, I believe in eating in moderation, but a large tub of popcorn quickly disappears in my presence when I am zoning out in front of a film.

My team members really enjoy doing UX work. Although our research is light touch and not particularly scientific, it does give us insight into who is using the spaces and how. We have captured quantitative data, which can be counted or measured, and qualitative data, which is more about opinions and emotions. Quantitative methods include surveys (closed questions), choice tests (e.g., clicks, chips in boxes, etc.), and people-counting. Qualitative methods include interviews, usability tests and focus groups (Stockwell, 2016). To understand who is using the space, we can capture user data, such as relevant demographic questions in surveys or in interviews (e.g., gender, ethnicity, course, course level).

At a previous institution we used a simple graffiti board where students could leave comments and recommendations about the space. This information, along with how the space was reconfigured daily by students, provided some useful insights. Students made recommendations about new equipment or software to be acquired. Continual clusters of chairs around electrical sockets told us that we needed to install more charge points. Constant disruption of staff space by students requesting equipment for loan told us that we needed to build a separate equipment store. Because at the time many students borrowed laptops, we captured information to understand which students from which courses tended to use the space when.

At another institution, a separate student centre with informal seating and study spaces was created in a rebuild. The expectation was that these new spaces would take the pressure off the main library, which got very busy during exam periods. There were teaching rooms on the upper floors of both the student centre and the building where the library was located. However, students continued to congregate in the flexible spaces in the main library because they wanted to remain close to the collections, while the informal spaces in the student centre were underutilised. Qualitative comments from students complaining about the lack of study spaces in the library provided clear evidence of student concerns. Staff members using the simple observational technique of comparing student use of the library and the student centre spaces at key times, such as exam periods and hand-ins, also provided insights. In the end, the library team created a campaign of 'Take a break, release the space' and signposted students to the informal spaces at the student centre to enjoy a snack and relax before hunkering down in the library again. We also controlled public access to the main library during peak times to prioritise our students. In retrospect, it might have been worth reducing the number of comfy areas in the main library to better differentiate it from the student centre's informal spaces. The access-control facility of the main library told us who was using the library, and when.

At my current institution, we wanted to understand how student space use had changed post COVID-19 restrictions. Even though we had returned to campus in 2022, all quantitative statistics indicated a reduction in usage: lower footfall, reduced loans, fewer in-person enquiries. In May of that year, we commissioned a colleague from our UX design team to do some research on both libraries to understand how students and academic staff were using the space post pandemic, and whether the existing zones still made sense. We also took the opportunity to explore with users how the spaces could be enhanced, including what technological resources were required.

As already mentioned, we had a range of quantitative statistics available to us, so the researcher focused on gathering qualitative data through focus groups and interviews with students and other stakeholders, including library and academic staff members. Students taking part in the research about the Docklands Library said they found the zoning difficult to understand and that noise bounces around due to hard surfaces. One academic described the difficulty of teaching in one of the open-plan teaching spaces in the Docklands Library (Burke, 2022), which were considered sector-leading when they were built more than 20 years earlier. For the Stratford Library, students expressed concern about the strain on access to study spaces. (See later in the chapter how this concern was exacerbated by other space changes at the Stratford Library prompted by institutional demands.) Students at Stratford also requested more collaborative spaces on the lower ground floor.

At the Docklands Library, we have implemented some signage solutions to better signpost zoning for students and have made signage accessible (e.g., using Navilens codes to help visually impaired students and staff to navigate spaces). Although the Docklands Library has some sound buffers, these have only limited effect, so further solutions need to be implemented. As ever, funding and estate prioritisation must be balanced. At the Stratford Library we were able to implement a tech-enhanced collaborative space, which was requested by and is popular among students.

National satisfaction surveys

In the higher education sector in the United Kingdom and Ireland, national satisfaction surveys are used to understand student experiences of universities. The National Student Survey (NSS) targets final-year undergraduates and is run on behalf of the Office for Students (OfS), the regulatory body for English universities. The Postgraduate Taught Education Survey (PTES) and the Postgraduate Research Experience Survey (PRES) are run by AdvanceHE, an international charity aimed at the development and improvement of higher education. The International Student Barometer (ISB), run by I-Graduate, captures feedback from international students. Generally, these surveys use a four- or five-point Likert scale of positive or negative comments such as 'Strongly agree' to 'Strongly disagree'. In 2023, the NSS moved to a four-point *Positivity* measure after consultation with the sector. Qualitative comments are also collected from participants in the survey. Table 3.2 lists survey questions related to libraries.

Table 3.2 *Library-related satisfaction questions*

NSS (2023)	How well have library resources (e.g., books, online services, and learning spaces) supported your learning? (OfS, 2023b)
PTES (2022)	There is appropriate access to physical library resources and facilities (Leman, 2022)
PRES (2023)	There is appropriate access to physical library resources and facilities (Neves, 2023)
ISB (2022)	The physical library facilities Online library (ISB, 2022)

The NSS question references *space*, whereas the remaining surveys reference *facilities*. It is the students' interpretation of what should be considered within the scope of the question. You must drill into the comments to see if there are details about the spaces. However, vague as these metrics are, they are key benchmarking tools for UK higher education institutions. The NSS score comprises part of the 'Learning Resources' score on the Teaching Excellence Framework (TEF), a scheme run by the OfS for continuous improvement in the delivery of courses and outcomes for students (OfS, 2023a). The other components of the 'Learning Resources' score are IT and course-specific resources, which can include anything from sewing machines for fashion students to CAD (Computer Aided Design) applications for architecture students. As the TEF looks at four years' worth of data, a low NSS score for the library-specific question, as with the other components, will impact on the TEF for the four-year period.

Although the above metrics are used as measures of success by universities, they lag by a year. To obtain current insights and to understand the extent to which spaces impact on these scores requires triangulation with other available information. What comments are made during course committee meetings, on module questionnaires, via feedback mechanisms for the libraries (e.g., chat, online feedback forms, social media, face-to-face at the helpdesk) or UX research? Only through analysing all this information can we understand if the space is fit for its current users.

And what of our future students? We need to go beyond our walls to understand how future students may use our libraries. Young people in our own families are an interesting point of insight. I sat, fascinated, watching my early-teens niece's fingers fly across her iPhone as she created and edited a TikTok video while giving me her opinion about life. We can see how students from our local feeder schools are using spaces – or whether they even have libraries – and the tools and technologies they are using. Ideally, we would facilitate focus groups to have targeted conversations with these potential students – or invite them in to experience our library spaces and observe how they navigate the spaces. Pre COVID-19, around GCSE and A-Level periods, we received requests from local pupils for access to quiet spaces to study. As already noted, however, we prioritise demand from our own students before allowing visitor access. At any rate, pupil requests dropped off during the start of the COVID-19 pandemic, due to the imposition of restrictions and changes to students' exams. Pupil requests for access to study space are resuming as the exam regime returns to normal.

When spaces collide: a case study

Wilson's *Places of Learning Spectrum* (Wilson, 2009) portrays spaces on a continuum from *unstructured*, such as home or park to *structured*, such as teaching and learning spaces or a lecture theatre. A traditional library would sit roughly in the middle of this continuum, with social learning spaces just to the left of centre. UEL's Stratford Library, like many modern libraries, provides a combination of these spaces, signposted by zones: noisy areas on the ground floor, quiet and silent zones on the upper floors. Generally, the zones have worked over the decade or so life of the library. As ever, students, particularly postgraduate students, continued to demand more dedicated study spaces, but the library worked. However, when events led to the close adjacency of unstructured and structured spaces, the library team had some thinking to do to make it work.

The writing on the wall

I was aware, when I joined the university in 2018 that the Stratford main campus needed to be re-planned and rejuvenated. Parts of the campus had been standing since the institution's inception in the late 19th century, with room configurations and labyrinthine corridors that made navigation difficult for students and staff. There were other, temporary buildings, portacabins really, that were reaching the end of their life and planning permission.

Conversely, the Stratford Library was built in 2013 and remains a modern facility popular among its users, according to student feedback, and the staff members who work there. So, it made sense that any planning for the campus would include the library building in some form; after all, why demolish a recently built, modern, functional building?

Prior to COVID-19, in 2019 some new programmes were coming on stream at Stratford main campus that meant an increase in student numbers and a demand for additional space. With some of the temporary buildings planned for decommissioning, there were few choices for where to comfortably place the incoming cohort of students. The computer centre, the main location for open access computers for students, was replaced with classrooms. Although there were complaints from academic staff whose courses relied on the computer centre, there was no uproar from the students. I saw this as an opportunity to increase the capacity of open access computers in the Stratford Library, and, to date, the libraries are the largest providers of open access computers in the university.

But the computer centre wasn't enough. More space was needed and the 'obvious' choice was the Stratford Library. The proposal was to convert all the open study spaces on the upper floors into teaching spaces, reducing the available study space for students. As already mentioned, previous UX work at Stratford Library indicated that students were requesting *more* not *less* space. Also, the closure of the computer centre had already reduced the available study spaces for students. Needless to say, my team and I were alarmed at the scale of the proposal.

The proposed changes would have meant that there would be no silent study until the teaching day concluded, which could be up to 9 pm during the week and until roughly 5 pm on Saturdays. The odd Sunday seminar could also be programmed. The remaining quiet study spaces would essentially be thoroughfares for access/egress and linger space for students and staff waiting to enter classrooms. Due to the tight schedule for completion of works, there was no time to re-plan the library, such as reconfiguration of the book stacks, furniture or benching.

After consultation with the campus library team, I met with the then Director of Estates to recommend some alternatives that would mitigate the impact on the student and staff experience. A key recommendation was to preserve a silent study floor on the upper level and rethink the zoning of the remaining spaces, while maintaining the ground floor with its group and snack spaces as the noisier floor. Further discussion with the timetabling team revealed that an additional classroom of about 30 spaces would meet the space demands for the incoming cohort. Student study spaces were spared – but for how long?

Two study rooms were combined to create a single, long classroom on the library's nosier ground floor. The health and safety team confirmed that there was sufficient linger space between the new classroom and the open access computers. The disability team confirmed that there was sufficient turning space for wheelchair users. Considering the scale of the initial proposal, my team and I felt that we could make this compromise work. Students could use the classroom when it was not timetabled. Facilities and the IT/AV (audiovisual) teams would manage the classroom environment as normal. The library team would manage noise and the residual impacts of access and egress to the room.

Use of the new classroom for teaching was slow to start, frustrating students seeking study spaces. At first students were reluctant to use the room for fear of being asked to leave. However, the library team reassured them about the times when the rooms could be used. The unfortunate reality was that the 30-seater room was being used by a few students at a time, so the space utilisation was not great.

A year later, the classroom was being used more consistently for teaching and student reluctance to use the room resurged. Students were reminded via signage and during inductions about when the classroom could be used for personal study.

Round two

Three years later, in 2022, further growth in student numbers was projected – which was great news for the university. Post COVID-19, hybrid working, learning and teaching was the norm. That is, both students and staff benefited from the use of technology to enable flexibility in how they worked and learned. Cue the estates team to assess space utilisation across all university assets, including the libraries. Any space analysis had to consider agreed changes to the working patterns of staff, or the type of spaces required to facilitate technology-enhanced active learning (TEAL), the agreed pedagogy of the institution. TEAL-enabled immersive learning requires spaces where students can solve real-world problems using tools and technology that are relevant to industry. There have been some impressive experiential learning spaces created across the university: a primary care unit where students practise using life-like mannequins, augmented reality and virtual reality to diagnose patients; a trading floor simulating financial markets; and a courtroom where students hold mock trials. The expectation was that any new classroom would have built-in flexibility and technology to facilitate TEAL.

Redevelopment of several spaces on the Stratford main campus was underway, with the development of immersive spaces. However, some works that would yield the envisioned expansion were still years away. The Stratford Library was not going to escape further space loss, in the circumstances.

The project management triangle

Having navigated the 2019 space change, I was acutely aware that library spaces are university spaces. As the leader responsible for service provision within the library spaces, I was keen to be kept informed of the estates master plan so that I could maintain the best possible experience for our students and staff. I visited various universities to see how structured classroom spaces can operate alongside less structured library and learning spaces, and shared insights from my site visits with the Stratford site development team. The University of Northampton (discussed in Chapter 9) was an obvious exemplar, as they were the UEL muse for active blended learning and developed their learning and teaching spaces around this pedagogy.

Notification that more Stratford Library student study spaces would be converted into teaching spaces came in the summer, about two weeks before work was to commence and with a works duration of 6–8 weeks to enable completion by the start of the new academic year. So began the first imbalance of the project management triangle: *time*. To meet the required deadline, there was no time to adequately consider the implications of the design. The *scope* of the project was to create classrooms using affordable materials that could be sourced quickly. As the contractors worked weekdays, weekends and bank holidays to meet the deadlines, the *cost* of the project would have been impacted. The triangle was not balanced, with the *quality* of the design and stakeholder relationships at risk.

I pulled as many levers as I could with executive leaders to encourage considered and holistic re-planning of the library spaces – with input from the local team – that would gain needed classrooms while mitigating loss of study spaces and an adverse student experience. One key lever was the potential adverse impact on NSS ratings, which would have a four-year impact on our TEF scores.

The project progressed and the open study spaces on the first and second floors were converted into teaching rooms, with some space retained for open access computing and group and individual study space. I undertook an Equality Impact Assessment (EIA), which highlighted ambient noise concerns that would adversely affect neurodivergent students and staff. In addition, the didactic configuration of the narrow classrooms raised concerns about the manoeuvrability of wheelchairs and the suitability for TEAL.

Although team morale was low, due to the lack of consultation, we got on with the business of making the spaces work for students and staff. We changed the zoning to quiet and collaborative spaces during teaching hours and maintained silent study on the upper floors after teaching. The vacant classrooms became silent study spaces. To achieve this, we initially had to block-book the classrooms to keep them free for students in the late evenings.

Although the building contractors tried to do noisy work during the early mornings, August and early September were disruptive months for students and staff during 2022. Earplugs were made available and we kept users informed of work progress. We also created a silent study area in another building as a haven for students. By the start of term in 2022, the construction of the teaching spaces had largely been completed with most IT/AV installed. Although there was the usual tail of snagging, the classrooms could be used.

Utilisation

The classrooms were built, but the teaching did not come initially. As with the classroom built in 2019, not much teaching took place in the first academic year, as other existing spaces sufficed. There was a missed opportunity to engage local staff and students about how to redevelop the spaces to meet the needs of the university.

What we observed over the first year was that individuals (most often) and small groups would close themselves in classrooms with 30 study spaces. Other students were reluctant to co-use the space for fear of conflict. Also, small groups of staff members would arrange meetings in these classrooms, often involving catering, whereas students were asked to use the snack area on the ground floor for eating. Neither represented good space utilisation. Predictably, students began to complain about the lack of study space.

To minimise the use of the classrooms as a meeting space for staff, I agreed with the catering team that no catering would be delivered to the library. I also wrote to academic colleagues asking them to use other meeting rooms around the university to preserve the classrooms for student study. Colleagues supported this request, as they were aware of students' concerns about the changes to the library spaces.

At the time of writing, we are well into the new academic year. Now that the teaching spaces were being used increasingly, we have found some need for adjustment. The estates team has had to revisit ventilation to accommodate the number of people in the classrooms. Lecturers had been teaching with the doors open to enable ventilation, thus increasing noise in the limited, adjacent student study areas. When teaching rooms are not booked, individual and small groups of students continue to barricade themselves in 30-seat rooms, requiring intervention from library and security staff. We are revisiting the UX research done pre-COVID-19 to fully understand the student experience of using the spaces.

Lessons learned for the next round

Use of the libraries has changed post pandemic restrictions, with footfall and face-to-face enquiries increasing after the decrease in 2021/22. The demand for space is a positive for the institution and we want our incoming students to have outstanding experiences while learning, studying and researching at the university. So, when the next round of space demands occurs, I will make it a priority to consult with stakeholders even if it is a rapid turnaround. Use of graffiti boards in the library and online pulse surveys outlining the challenge and soliciting ideas for solutions could be fun ways of engaging users. A task and finish group of library team members brainstorming ideas and canvassing opinions will enable staff members to feel more involved. A tight turnaround will limit the level of engagement, but some input from stakeholders is better than none.

In my effort to protect the student spaces and experience, I may have appeared less collegiate than desirable by highlighting more problems than solutions. There is a fine balance here, as my team and I understand how the spaces operate, and so we were vocal in raising concerns about decisions that would have an adverse collateral impact.

Finally, I suspected that the Stratford Library would come back into the frame after 2019 as space demands persisted. As a member of the university management board, I expected to learn of any space developments in that forum. However, the forum had been completed for the academic year and the emerging space demands came during the summer, when most staff members were looking forward to a holiday. I know now to keep asking questions about estates plans and to keep to hand some high-level recommendations about space development, informed by stakeholder input.

Conclusion

Library leaders must have clear sight of the estates master plan for their institution. They can then ensure that their services align with the master plan, and continually assess whether the spaces designed meet the university's needs. Of course, internal or external drivers may necessitate a deviation from the strategy, but clear and timely cross-institution communication would enable services to work together to deliver solutions. Ideally, the project management triangle of cost, scope and time would be balanced to enable seamless delivery of quality spaces. The Stratford Library case study illustrated a misalignment of time and scope which impacted on the outcome for the spaces and stakeholder relationships. The library and estates and facilities teams must work together to implement solutions to make spaces work and to preserve a positive UX for current and future users.

References

Burke, E. (2022) Library Space User Experience, University of East London, p. 11.

I-Graduate (2022) International Student Barometer University of East London 2022 Wave 2 (internal report).

Leman, J. (2022) Postgraduate Taught Experience Survey 2022: Findings for the Sector, AdvanceHE, www.advance-he.ac.uk/knowledge-hub/postgraduate-taught-experience-survey-2022.

Moreland, B. (2014) What Are Space Frequency, Occupancy, and Utilisation Rates and How Do I Calculate Them, https://educationspaceconsultancy.com/what-are-space-frequency-occupancy-and-utilisation-rates-and-how-do-i-calculate-them.

Neves, J. (2023) Postgraduate Research Experience Survey 2023: Sector Results Report, AdvanceHE, www.advance-he.ac.uk/knowledge-hub/postgraduate-research-experience-survey-2023.

Office for Students (2023a) About the Teaching Excellence Framework, www.officeforstudents.org.uk/advice-and-guidance/the-tef/about-the-tef.

Office for Students (2023b) NSS Questionnaire, www.officeforstudents.org.uk/media/c2ddb4c1-34cf-4df4-8c26-b6469412768f/nss-2023-questionnaire.pdf.

RIBA (2020) Post Occupancy Evaluation: An Essential Tool for the Built Environment, www.architecture.com/knowledge-and-resources/resources-landing-page/post-occupancy-evaluation-an-essential-tool-to-improve-the-built-environment.

Rudder, A. and Main, K. (2023) What is the Project Management Triangle? *Forbes*, www.forbes.com/advisor/business/project-management-triangle.

Stockwell, A. (2016) UX Foundations: Research, linkedin.com/learning/ux-foundations-research-19417883.

University of East London Library, Archives, and Learning Services (LALS) (2023) LALS Usage Data Report 2022–23 (internal document).

Wilson, H. (2009) The Process of Creating Learning Space. In Radcliffe, D., Wilson, H., Powell, D. and Tibbetts, B. (eds) *Learning Spaces in Higher Education: Positive Outcomes by Design. Proceedings of the Next Generation Learning Spaces 2008 Colloquium, University of Queensland*, University of Queensland, www.academia.edu/10392806/Learning_Spaces_in_Higher_Education_Positive_Outcomes_by_Design.

4

A Practical Guide to Writing a Successful Business Case to Influence University Estates Strategy

Anna O'Neill

Introduction

As access to funding becomes increasingly competitive, with ever closer scrutiny to ensure wise investment and value for money, writing an internal business case is now an essential skill across all areas of library practice. But I believe it is also an area where libraries can leverage their unique position. At the nexus of professional services and the faculty, library business cases can be well placed to garner wide support, deliver on multiple agendas and strategies and derive maximum benefit.

However, faced with a blank sheet of virtual paper, writing a business case can feel a daunting task. This chapter aims to demystify the process and provide an outline of the key steps and considerations needed to make a great idea happen or to address a known need. This guidance can apply to any area of library work, including building projects, new or replacement technology, increased staff resource, a change in the delivery of a service or a new way of working. And it is of course likely that, with many estates-related projects, all of the above will be included.

The need for a business case

There are many reasons why an argument for a change or new course of action might be proposed, but before a business case is started I find it helpful to consider some key questions, such as the following.

- Is there an identifiable benefit for the organisation?
- Is there a good reason or clear drivers for the change being proposed?
- What options have been considered?
- Are the costs and the benefits clear?
- Who are the key stakeholders and what is their interest in the proposal?
- Have assumptions been tested and the required evidence gathered?

If your answer to the first two questions is 'yes', then the answer to the remaining questions will form the basis to justify resources or expenditure for your proposal. Your business case should provide all the information needed to allow key decision makers to come to an informed decision about funding the project and to clarify the benefits that will be realised.

How to get started

In my experience it is important to be clear about the governance route for a business case; that is, how a decision will be made. In complex organisations like universities, decision making and governance can be quite opaque, with both academic and corporate governance (as defined below by AdvanceHE) playing roles – and in the case of the library, there is likely to be a requirement to satisfy both routes.

> The term 'academic governance' refers to how the academic matters of the institution are governed. Typically, academic governance will cover matters such as student admissions, academic standards and academic quality. By contrast 'corporate governance' normally describes areas such as finance and estates. Together 'academic' and 'corporate' governance form the system of governance for most higher education institutions (HEIs).
>
> (AdvanceHE, 2023)

I have found that it is worth spending time to understand the route that will need to be taken and where decisions will need to be made. The larger the request, the more likely it is that there will be multiple stages and a range of stakeholders, with the timing of approval committees or deadlines dictated by the university calendar. Planning ahead will help to ensure that a slot on a busy agenda can be found, and provides the writer of the business case with key deadlines.

Once it is clear what route the business case will need to take, it is likely that there will be a template for each stage of approval. Depending on the project and the number of stages of approval there may be several different templates. This layering of approval may feel onerous, but it is designed to reduce workload, with shorter papers at the beginning providing both the writer and readers (i.e., stakeholders and decision makers) a quick and effective means of getting a sense of the project/request and either moving it to the next stage or asking for further information. Table 4.1 opposite provides a guide to the titles that these templates are sometimes given.

While this may seem like a lot of work before getting started in earnest, it has the invaluable benefit of beginning the process of socialisation; that is, talking about, sharing and discussing, with a wide range of stakeholders, what

Table 4.1 *Example template names and stages of approval from three universities where the author has worked*

Stage of approval (if more than one)	Examples of template names
Stage 1	Pre-concept paper Statement of need Initial qualification assessment
Stage 2	Concept paper Options appraisal Outline business case
Stage 3	Business case

it is hoped to achieve. This approach also acknowledges that complex organisations have both formal and informal governance routes. While a university committee and decision-making structure provides the formal governance route for a business case, the informal governance recognises the softer, cultural aspect of the decision-making process. This approach also accepts that most universities place value on the discursive nature of their organisations, and also appreciate the joint endeavour that is undertaken to deliver higher education and the multiplicity of voices and activities that come together to create and deliver education and research.

Begin with why

In order to write a compelling business case, it is essential to be clear about both the issue it will resolve and the future vision that you are driving towards. It is important to be able to clearly articulate the 'why' before beginning to think about the 'what' or 'how'. It can help to think of this as the story behind the proposal. In his book *Start with Why* (Sinek, 2011), Simon Sinek provides a range of evidence to support starting with this approach.

While it may seem obvious to you that essential work needs to be done, or that a high-volume use building like a library needs investment, it is what happens in the building and the impact on the people who use it that will bring to life the 'why' of the case and help stimulate support. Consider from the start what positive benefits the investment would bring to the users of the space and the opportunities it presents for the future. A SWOT (strengths, weaknesses, opportunities and threats) analysis can be a useful starting point, as it can help the business case writer clarify the problem or objective, and often generates alternatives and options. For the business case reader, a SWOT analysis as shown in Figure 4.1 on the next page can help to highlight, summarise and focus attention on the key issues.

The story or narrative that is being created should link back to the institution's strategy, whether that is a departmental strategy, the education

Strengths	Weaknesses
• Centrally located building with extended opening hours • Good study/learning environment management • Responsiveness to requests from students and academic colleagues • Good relationships with academic departments and professional services colleagues • Expert staff • Recognised for good financial management	• National satisfaction scores consistently below sector • Poor user journey to access digital services • Libraries and study spaces have not been developed in line with university growth – no plans in the pipeline • Inconsistent accessibility across library spaces • Insufficient understanding of academic/student journey • Insufficient engagement with local community and outside organisations
Opportunities	**Threats**
• Improvement in national and internal satisfaction scores • Improved student and academic journey • Ringfenced funding for improving environmental standards across the estate • Potential to increase the number of learning spaces in related estates projects • Realignment of office spaces across campus through hybrid working could release additional space for independent study	• Perception that library services are focused on undergraduate students • Perception that increase of 'commuter students' reduces the need for space • Significant increase in inflation (particularly energy costs) undermines institutional capacity for investment into recurrent costs • Committed spend to support development in this area reduces the capacity for investment in other areas • Recruitment and retention issues causing lack of capacity within professional service teams

Figure 4.1 *A generic library SWOT analysis*

or research strategy or the university strategy. It should resonate for the organisation and align with the key drivers for the institution at that moment. To really understand what those drivers are, and in order to build support, a thorough and comprehensive understanding of the audience for the business case is needed.

How to build support

No business case should be submitted cold. It is vital to confer, discuss, explore and exchange ideas about the proposal being articulated and to cultivate support before writing anything down. There is no short cut. In my experience, the lack of time spent at this stage will almost certainly lead to a poorer result or long-term delays.

Early socialisation has numerous benefits. It will help to:

- ensure alignment with institutional drivers;
- understand the less-known or informal priorities of the institution;

- understand both formal and informal decision making;
- test the 'why' and get feedback on whether it is convincing;
- provide alternative considerations or arguments and challenge any assumptions or bias;
- clarify the governance route for the case if it is not clear.

It is therefore also worth identifying and engaging with the forums or meetings that involve the broader community so as to ensure maximum community inclusion and to acknowledge the significance and influence of roles that sit outside of formal governance structures. Consider those people who can act as champions and advocates (e.g., estates team, departmental administrators, personal assistants, liaison librarians and finance business partners). Alternatively, it could be useful to design a facilitated event which can be used to help set the objectives for your case, ideate options and benefits, share and/or understand concerns and fears and identify any potential points of conflict. The value of corridor conversations, coffee-queue chats and end-of-meeting catch-ups is not to be overlooked. The digital equivalent could include messaging technology, side chats in online meetings or speedy online calls.

If there appears to be a lack of support at this stage, it could simply be a matter of timing, or that there is a more pressing need; but the feedback and discussion will make this evident. And, while it may be disappointing not to receive the interest hoped for, it will likely have saved a great deal of wasted effort. Limited support at this stage will almost certainly undermine and probably lead to the ultimate failure of a business case.

It is easy to rush or overlook this stage, but it is a fundamental component of a successful business case. Knowing your audience and engaging with your stakeholder community is key, and is a theme we will return to multiple times throughout this chapter.

Understand your audience and their motivations

In order to present the benefits and opportunities that will be delivered by the case being made, it is essential to understand what is important to the identified audience and to acknowledge that approaches might need to be changed and adapted, depending on governance routes.

Change has become a constant in higher education, so it is also important to consider what changes might be happening or are being planned within the institution. Because these will likely create new strategies or drive an institution's future direction and focus, your business case should take them into account.

Begin by thinking about the link between what you plan to achieve and the university's strategy, as this is the clearest driver for new developments and the investment of resources. It will also ensure that the business case is linked to and sits within the context of wider institutional strategies and will have a positive influence on delivering those strategies. Without a very clear link and joining between strategy and case, it is likely the case won't make it through the first hurdle, or that further work will be requested. Depending on the university, the focus of the strategy may vary. However, some examples of things that are likely to be important include:

- stated institutional aims for growth or diversification of student market;
- variety of provision, e.g., apprenticeships, online delivery, distance learning;
- league tables and rankings;
- student experience;
- research impact;
- civic/regional engagement;
- innovation/enterprise;
- value for money/invest to save/cost reduction;
- compliance and risk;
- change driven by government policy or regulation;
- technological opportunity;
- external real-world or geopolitical events.

It should become clear from some detailed reading of the relevant strategies within your university where the focus is, and it is also worth noting what business cases are being agreed at the time, as they will also indicate where investment is being made.

Undertaking a stakeholder analysis at this stage will define the audience for the business case and help in understanding their potential influence and the best means of engagement. There are different models for this type of analysis, but in my experience the 'power/interest matrix' shown in Figure 4.2 opposite has been the most useful. Adapted from Mendelow 1991, the matrix allows you to plot your stakeholders on a grid to determine who has high or low power to affect your project, and who has high or low interest. Your approach can then be adapted for each quadrant as described below.

High power, high interest: These stakeholders are likely to be decision makers and can have the biggest impact on the project's success. You need to keep these stakeholders close, to manage their expectations.

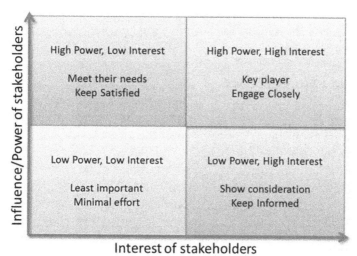

Figure 4.2 *Power/interest matrix used to analyse individual stakeholders by measuring their interest and influence/power* (adapted from Mendelow, 1991).

High power, low interest: These stakeholders need to be kept informed on what is happening on the project. Even though they may not be interested in the outcome, their power means that they are influential. These types of stakeholders should be dealt with cautiously, as they could use their power in a negative way if they become dissatisfied.

Low power, high interest: Keep these people adequately informed and talk to them to ensure that no major issues are arising. These people can often be very helpful with the detail and delivery of your project.

Low power, low interest: Monitor these people, but do not spend time and energy on excessive communication.

It is tempting to focus on the high power, high interest quadrant – but remember, too, the point made earlier about informal governance and decision making. For example, those colleagues who have high power and low interest might need to be encouraged to take a greater interest in order to facilitate the progress of your business case – not least because their higher-interest areas may direct funding away from your business case and block a positive decision. In addition, valued colleagues who may come into the low power, high interest quadrant – for example cleaning and maintenance staff – will be crucial to the successful delivery and ongoing benefits of the case to the organisation.

If it is not clear or straightforward what your audience is interested in, spend the time needed to introduce your plans and to get to know them.

This will have the added benefit of expanding your network, allowing you to practise the narrative around the case for investment and test its impact and effect.

Gathering your evidence

Evidence is a vital component in building the argument that underpins a business case. It is also pivotal in growing support, demonstrating need and clarifying the benefits and opportunities of the project or programme. It can often seem that the case for change is self-evident, particularly if an issue presents as a 'burning platform' – i.e., a problem that simply cannot be ignored. However, identifying the root cause of a problem, not just the symptom, is essential to ensuring a robust case.

Universities keep a watchful eye on league tables and rankings, so comparison data can be useful to provide qualitative evidence. Most universities have a 'competitor basket' (this is often a mix of universities with a similar mission or size, based on locality or that are held in esteem) and it is worthwhile including some data which includes this group.

It may also be possible to draw on established data sets. In the UK and Ireland, a well-used data set is the SCONUL (Society of College, National and University Libraries) Statistics (www.access.sconul.ac.uk/page/sconul-statistics), which provides an annual insight into the collections, services and activities of its members and can be a useful starting point. Similar international datasets are also available, and it may be possible to exploit relevant sector networks to acquire the data needed. Figure 4.3 opposite shows an example data set comparing the home university to others.

It is also important to ensure that you have evidence of the benefits and added value to your user community and the wider organisation. It is worth mining for both qualitative and quantitative information through local or national survey results; for instance, an internal student satisfaction or staff engagement survey or, in the UK the National Student Survey, Postgraduate Taught Experience Survey or Postgraduate Research Experience Survey.

Creating your own points of engagement with stakeholders, for example by carrying out your own survey or focus groups and interviews, will provide rich data on the value that could be created. This will help to articulate the benefit of the investment being requested and the value it will return. An example of how to measure the social return of investment for an academic library is detailed in *ADP Architecture Insights* (White, 2023).

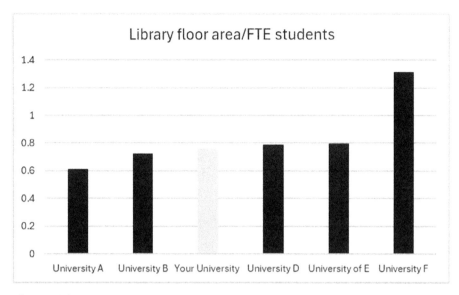

Figure 4.3 *Library floor area (m²) per FTE student could be used to compare the home university library to other university libraries* (data from SCONUL Statistics 2021–22).

Start writing

Once the point of writing arrives, be aware that if you use a template, it can be prescriptive about what information is required and the format and length. In some cases, the key decision maker(s) may have strong views or preferences about how they want the information presented. Understanding how best to present your case can be key to obtaining a positive decision. For example, presenting a lot of data to a decision maker who prefers a narrative presentation (or vice versa) might undermine your chances of getting the result you want. I have found that committee secretaries or administrators are a good first point of contact to find out if a particular template is required and to check if there are any preferences or institutional norms that should be taken into consideration.

Whatever the template (or even if there is no template), it is important that the business case has a compelling argument and clear reasoning; one that starts with and highlights 'why' the investment or change is needed before, moving on to the 'how'.

Any facts and data presented will need to be evidence based and as objective as possible. If it appears that data has been manipulated or something obvious has been excluded, the credibility of the entire business case risks being undermined. Powerful visuals, for example, charts, images or easy-to-understand tables, will add strength to the argument.

Be a considerate author and recognise the time pressure that most people feel in their professional lives. Include an executive summary and clearly outline any recommendations at the start. Use headings and bullet points to guide readers through the document and be as clear and concise as possible. The following are typical headed sections:

- title page, including author, version number, date;
- contents page;
- short executive summary making clear what decision is needed;
- short background description of the current situation or relevant past events;
- requirement, and the case for change;
- clear benefits analysis;
- appraisal of the options available and those discounted;
- resourcing requirements, e.g., what project costs are needed to start the business case;
- dependencies, or elements of the proposal that rely on the completion or delivery of something else;
- risk analysis, to highlight and rate uncertainty or potential negative outcomes;
- key milestones/timescales: the expected timeline and key decision points.

Executive summary

An executive summary needs to be concise but cover the key points. It is often useful to leave this section to last, so that you can more easily draw out the key information you have included in your plan. No more than a few paragraphs long, the executive summary should include a brief outline of the current position, the problem or opportunity being addressed, objectives, key findings, benefits and recommendations.

Options considered/options appraisal

Many business cases will ask for an 'options appraisal' which provides a useful means to demonstrate that wider thinking and research has taken place and that the business case has been contextualised. An options appraisal might include:

- doing nothing/maintaining the status quo;
- stopping an activity;
- options which make clear the benefits return for differing levels of investment or scope;
- radical options (relocation, significantly different operating model, etc.).

Every option should give clear and concise factual information, for example, about the time, cost, benefits, advantages, disadvantages, risks and constraints of alternatives. This allows options to be compared from a balanced viewpoint. The 'do nothing' option should always be included to demonstrate what would happen if no change was pursued.

The presentation of the different options requires some care. Decision makers will need to be convinced that while robust consideration has been given to alternatives, the option being recommended is indeed the most compelling. It can sometimes be worth considering an options appraisal early on, as thinking about alternative scenarios can help in creating a strong business case.

An example of an options appraisal is given in Figure 4.4 on the next page. They can be visual or written options, or detailed cost options. In my experience, this is a key opportunity to use your knowledge of the presentation preferences of the key decision maker(s).

Benefits

Benefits can be both tangible and intangible, but should link to both your 'why' and the SWOT analysis, as well as to your institution's goals. They are sometimes described as a return on the investment (ROI) being made. This is often thought of as a financial return, but, as this can be limited for a library, in my experience it is helpful to also draw out the 'social' return (Table 4.2). Where a financial return is expected or can be proven, it is helpful to spell out the actual amounts over a given period.

Table 4.2 *Examples of financial and social return on investment*

Benefits/ROI	Financial	Social
Improvements to accessibility, usability and user satisfaction	Positive recommendation from current students supports future recruitment and fee income £X over X number of years	Enhances accessibility and equity for disabled users, reduces stress and supports well-being
Investment in building fabric to upgrade lighting, improve temperature control and reduce heat loss	Reduced maintenance costs £X over X number of years	Ability to adjust lighting in different spaces to support the needs of neurodiverse students; improved study environment supports academic success
Improved quality of staff working spaces improves staff satisfaction and retention	Improved staff attendance at work, reduces costs for temporary cover, reduces costs for advertising and recruitment £X over X number of years	Improved staff well-being and engagement enhances service provision

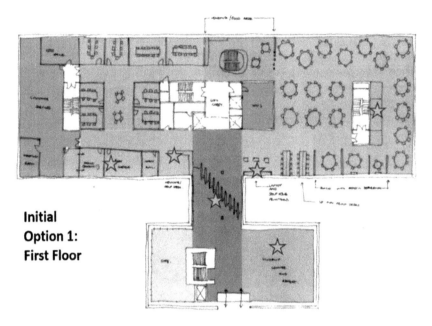

**Initial
Option 1:
First Floor**

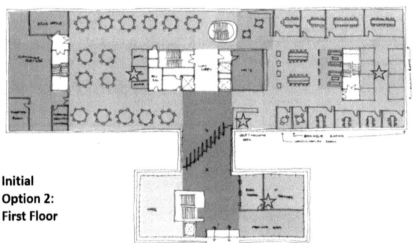

**Initial
Option 2:
First Floor**

Figure 4.4 *Different options for the layout of desks and individual study spaces
considered as part of a business case*

I have found that it is often the social ROI that brings to life the real value
of a project. Some of the ways in which this impact and value can be
highlighted are covered later, in the section on evidence. Benefits that
provide both a social and a financial ROI will have an obviously positive
impact on decision making.

Dependencies

This section of the business case should make clear if there are any relationships or interconnections between different projects or programmes, or if the case is dependent on an outcome, assumption or external factor such as a regulation, policy or market condition.

I have experienced various dependencies that sometimes were straightforward and relatively easy to address, sometimes outside of your control, and occasionally complex with various interdependencies. However, the real work of managing them comes later, so at this stage they are included to ensure that they have been captured and acknowledged, recognising that no project sits in isolation and allowing some visibility to the key points of interconnections with other activity within and outside the university. Some examples are:

- planning permission or building regulations being agreed;
- assumptions about recruitment targets being met;
- related IT infrastructure being in place, or the ability to put it in place;
- government policy remaining the same or changing in the way imagined;
- another project finishing on time (to release resources to deliver your project);
- availability of materials or supplies;
- results of investigations being positive (asbestos surveys, flood surveys, etc.);
- cost predictions (interest rate stability, oil prices, etc.).

Risks

The business case should also include a risk analysis. Risks may be based on prior experience, perceived likely outcomes or uncertainty if there is little or no history to provide a guide. Examples of sources of risk include:

- sole suppliers where there is no quick or easy alternative;
- unique materials, both the supply and price;
- lead times and/or timescales;
- legal requirements and compliance, e.g., planning permissions, building regulations;
- reputation;
- quality or availability of the time of key staff and management;
- timescale in relation to dependencies.

Major sources of risk are those over which you have little or no control, whereas minor risks tend to be areas where there are clear options and feasible possibilities to manage the risk. A template as shown in Table 4.3 can be used to display the potential risks. From experience, I have found that mitigations and controls are best endeavours. For example, my attempt to engage the local community in the future plans for a building stoked enough interest to generate an application to list it as a historic building. While certainly not the intention, it did amplify the need to address the building's issues with some urgency.

Table 4.3 *Example risk template*

Risk	Evaluation		Mitigation/control measures
	Likelihood	Impact	
	High Medium Low	High Medium Low	
Building is of historic interest and will have extensive planning requirements	x	x	Early engagement with planning authorities and local community
Excessive price inflation for required building materials	x	x	Additional contingency spend factored into budget, orders to be placed early in the project, close contact maintained with suppliers to track any anticipated major fluctuations
Reduction in study spaces during development and refurbishment	x	x	Additional study spaces to be provided elsewhere on campus

Costs and funding

Often, the most daunting part of putting together a business case can be dealing with the financial aspects. It can help to begin with small steps such as undertaking an options appraisal, feasibility study or some basic scoping work that requires a relatively modest budget. This will help to grow your familiarity and confidence with the financial components and can have the added benefit of enabling you to talk more knowledgeably and confidently when trying to inform or influence others.

Engage and collaborate with internal colleagues to gather the support and information required for the case that is being made. Estates colleagues, for instance, will be able to support pulling together the different stages of costing for a building project and can bring in some additional support in the form of a project manager and/or a quantity surveyor, which will help to build a robust cost base. Finance colleagues will be able to provide expertise in formatting and presenting financial information and IT colleagues can advise on technical infrastructure costs. Procurement colleagues will be key allies throughout the project. Earlier stakeholder analysis should identify key colleagues who can develop, support and understand the project, its timescales and future needs.

Financial data will need to be presented as clearly as possible, with as many costs included as possible, most likely over a three to five year period and always including VAT if applicable (Table 4.4). While it may be possible to do some of this early work within the library, financial colleagues will be in a much better position to provide this data in a clear and accurate way.

Table 4.4 *Example financial options appraisal showing the total cost over a fixed term and ongoing costs*

Occupancy software	Option A	Option B	Option C
Year 1	£53,760	£92,000	£120,000
Year 2	£20,160	£20,000	£25,000
Year 3	£20,160	£20,000	£25,000
Year 4	£20,160	£20,000	£25,000
Hardware costs over 3 years	£3,750	Included above	Included above
Total for 4 years	£117,990	£152,000	£195,000
Ongoing costs year 5 onwards	£20,160	£20,000	£25,000

It's been agreed, what happens next?

Once the business case has been agreed, it is time to move from theory to practice. A first step will be to create a governance mechanism (such as a steering group or project board) to help deliver the vision that has been set out. The scale of this will depend on the project but it should include key stakeholders identified during the mapping stage as having 'high power, high interest' (see Figure 4.2), and also expert colleagues and 'internal' stakeholders from the library team. The time needed to be devoted to the project needs to be clear to all members in order to manage expectations and to ensure the required level of engagement.

Depending on the scale of the project, the formality of the structure around project delivery may vary. In most cases, however, it is likely that a project manager will be allocated and a project board will be established.

The standard process in a particular institution will determine the next steps; however, it is also useful to consider how you will manage the project within the library. I have found it very helpful to identify an internal project lead who will be the key point of operational contact for the formal project manager, estates and procurement colleagues and library staff.

The project board will be accountable for the success of the project and have the authority to direct the project within the remit set by the university. It is also responsible for communications between the project management team and the stakeholders external to that team.

According to the scale, complexity, importance and risk of the project, the size of the project board and membership may vary. A project board will usually be composed as follows.

- **Project sponsor:** ultimately accountable for the success or failure of the project and must ensure that the project is focused on achieving its business objectives and delivering the stated benefits. This role is normally undertaken by someone operating at a senior level within the organisation, and often someone who sits outside of the library (depending on the project, this may be at university executive board level).
- **Project manager:** runs the project from day to day on behalf of the project sponsor. This role ensures that the project deliverables are of the required quality, i.e., are capable of delivering the benefits defined in the business case and produced within the agreed time and cost.
- **Senior user:** represents those groups who will use or gain benefit from the project and must be empowered to make decisions on their behalf (e.g., students, academics, etc.).
- **Senior supplier:** represents those groups who will design, develop, facilitate, procure and implement the project and must be empowered to make decisions on their behalf.
- **Procurement adviser:** provides professional advice and guidance for the procurement elements of the project.

I have found that it can be less daunting to break down the project into manageable chunks or shorter 'mini'-projects. This can be an effective way of delivering at pace, showing impact and benefits along the way and counteracting change or project fatigue. This approach also provides the potential of delivering at least some short-term project benefits to the cohort of students who would miss out on a project's longer-term values and impacts.

Even at this early stage, a communication and engagement plan is strongly recommended (Table 4.5 opposite). This will provide a framework to ensure

Table 4.5 *Shortened example of a stakeholder communication plan*

Stakeholder group	Why (the reason they are being communicated with)	What (key messages)	How (channel)	When (frequency, key dates etc.)	Who (who will convene/ present/ write)
Students' Union	Understand benefits and pain points, ensure proposal meets needs	Invitation for engagement and input, co-creation and support	Focus groups, surveys, forums	Monthly and ad hoc	Library senior leadership team
Staff/student liaison committees	Key users/ student representatives	Regular updates, requests for feedback	Committee agenda	As scheduled	Liaison librarians with input from project manager
Estates maintenance colleagues	Gain support for proposal, understanding of key maintenance issues that need to be addressed or factored in	Input and expertise	Regular meetings	Monthly	Library project lead
IT infrastructure team	Gain support for proposal, understanding of key IT issues that need to be addressed or factored in	Input and expertise	Regular meetings	Monthly	Library project lead

regular, appropriate and timely communications to all stakeholders and can also help to get buy-in from a range of colleagues who will often have competing priorities for any funding available.

Why do business cases fail to get agreed?

Universities work in a challenging and fluctuating financial landscape with finite resources that are in high demand. There are many reasons why even the most compelling and well-written business case is not funded. It may be that there are more urgent institutional requirements that address issues perceived as higher risk or that are a mandatory compliance issue. Sometimes it could be a matter of timing; for example, a change in institutional priorities that has not yet filtered through and manifested into strategies. I have found that in considering when to make or resubmit your business case, using the mnemonic PESTEL provides a structured framework to help you think about the current environment, as below.

- **Political:** What are the current government priorities; is there an election coming; do plans align with current or emerging policies internally or externally; what part of the organisation is being particularly favoured; where is investment being made?
- **Economic:** What are the current economic conditions; is financial performance good; is the institution looking at growth or seeking to reduce costs; what are the demographic trends that may impact on student numbers?
- **Social:** What social trends and interests are dominant at this time, e.g., well-being, mental health, flexible working, issues relating to equality and diversity; what is culturally important to the institution?
- **Technological:** What technology is being used and what is coming, e.g., digitisation and personalisation, the metaverse and AI; what are the generational differences in how people access, use and absorb information?
- **Environmental:** What environmental legislation and concerns are prevalent, in relation either to environmental protection or to business ethics?
- **Legal:** What are the legal compliance, social justice or new policies and practices that may be impacted on by internal or external pressures?

And, of course, asking for feedback on the reasons why a business case has been rejected will also help to clarify what would need to be addressed in the future or whether there is a better time to resubmit the case.

My very strong belief is that the key factor in improving the chances of a successful outcome is extensive consultation on and socialisation of the key concepts of the business case so as to get early and extensive engagement and support. This is critical in developing and conveying the benefits and value of the proposal. So, whatever your business case, start talking about it as early as possible, listen closely to the feedback you receive and ensure that you have explored and included the key benefits to your stakeholders and the university.

Conclusion

Every time I write a business case, I learn an enormous amount about my organisation and its formal and informal structures. The process allows me to create the space to think above and beyond normal service delivery, to consider the impact of external forces and to clarify the value of our library services and its benefits. Whether successful or not, I believe that writing a business case is never a wasted effort. The work you will do to understand and talk to your key stakeholders and professional services colleagues will have benefits across many other areas of your working life, creating connections, forging links and raising the visibility of your service and its goals and objectives.

References

AdvanceHE (2023) Academic Governance and Quality, www.advance-he.ac.uk/guidance/governance/getting-governance/governor-responsibilities/academic-governance-and-quality.

Mendelow, A. L. (1991) Environmental Scanning: The Impact of the Stakeholder Concept. In Patnaik, L. M. and Venugopal, K. R. (eds) *Proceedings from the Second International Conference on Information Systems, Cambridge, MA*.

Sinek, S. (2011) *Start with Why: How Great Leaders Inspire Everyone to Take Action*, Penguin Books.

White, T. (2023) Social Return on Investment (SROI) at the Laidlaw Library, *ADP Architecture Insights*, 26 July, https://adp-architecture.com/social-return-on-investment-sroi-at-the-laidlaw-library.

5

'Selling' the University: The Role of the Academic Library

Regina Everitt

Introduction

My son visited his mates in their first year of university. Upon his return, I was keen to hear what they thought about the campus. Having been to the University for a meeting, I was aware that it had a large, modern library with fantastic courtyard views over lush gardens. Although one of my university libraries has a wonderful view overlooking the Royal Albert Docks in London, I confess to having a bit of garden envy.

'Good weekend?' I asked. 'Yeah, good,' he said in near-monosyllabic detail.

'They have a great library,' I said, foraging for a more textured response. He is used to excitement about libraries from me. He has what I hope are fond memories of whiling away the time in the children's section in the local public library, flipping through picture books.

'Oh, I don't even think they know where that is,' he laughed.

Well, it's there when they discover they need it, I thought to myself. Unsurprisingly, in the heady, early days of university life, the 'perceived value' of the university library may not be obvious to some students. However, as course demands set in (such as the need for learning resources, study spaces and research skills development), the library's value comes to the fore. Bain & Company Inc. identify 30 elements of value for customers, and group them on a pyramid in four categories: functional, emotional, life changing and social impact – like Maslow's hierarchy of needs (Almquist et al., 2016). The functional or lowest rung of the ladder covers basic needs. Progressing up the ladder, next is the emotional rung, which includes rewards, wellness – something of personal value. The next rung up is life-changing, which includes belonging or motivation. The top rung is social impact. Initially, the library may meet the basic student need of providing a place to study – the bottom, functional rung. However, as the student progresses in their work and maturity, they may find that the library provides life-changing experiences.

Although few (if any) students will choose a university based on its library, they certainly will complain if they *don't* have a library or learning resource centre to support their studies. A great course or a renowned academic may initially attract a student to a university, but a great library may be among the reasons why the student *stays* at the university. So, the library plays an important role in 'selling' the university. And, like all assets that comprise the university 'product,' the library requires continual investment to keep attracting and retaining students.

In this chapter I will explore how academic libraries help to sell the university. 'Library' in this chapter refers to standalone or integrated physical spaces that may include physical books, study spaces, collaborative or social spaces, computer labs, makerspaces, etc. It is noted that many institutions have a range of study spaces that complement those within libraries.

Recruitment and retention

Prospective students

Libraries played an important role in my formative years. My local public library was a haven from my inner-city neighbourhood, particularly when long, hot summers pushed the tempers of bored youths to boiling point. My secondary school also had good library provision, where I enjoyed a creative writing workshop delivered by famous poet Sonya Sanchez. When I eventually applied to university, I just *assumed* that I would have access to a good library because I had such provision in my neighbourhood. The course (and discount for studying within my home state) attracted me to the university, but campus facilities, including the library, enhanced my time there.

Of course, as evidenced by my son's mates, a good library is unlikely to be at the top of the list for many prospective students. However, student advice resources do advise them to consider the university facilities, including the libraries, when making their final decision. The *Complete University Guide* tells students to consider 'how recently the university invested in resources such as libraries', noting how 'these facilities can improve students' learning experience and provide them with skills for employment' (Mosse, 2024). *What Uni* lists university facilities among the top ten things to compare when looking at universities (Smith, 2023). And *The Student Room Uni Guide* recommends that students review satisfaction scores like the National Student Survey (NSS) in the United Kingdom (UK) and Ireland and consider specific ratings for the university, including available facilities (Gardner, 2023).

As I had access to and positive experiences of using libraries, I understood the benefits of the availability of the facility. However, according to the National Literacy Trust, a quarter of disadvantaged primary schools in the

UK have no library and there is no government requirement for primary schools to have one (National Literacy Trust, 2021). Research commissioned by the Great School Libraries campaign, which advocates for equitable access to school libraries in the UK to impact positively on young people's life chances, found that, across the UK, disadvantaged students and/or students in rural areas either are less likely to have access to a library or have access to a library with limited resources. They are also less likely to have access to a dedicated librarian or library staff (Park, 2023). So, unless someone within their family or community has had experience of benefiting from a school or local library, it may not cross their mind as a 'selling point' for a university.

One morning, I found a home UK student wandering around one of the University of East London (UEL) libraries. When I asked her if she needed help, she said that she was just looking to see where things were, as she had never been in a library before. She seemed amazed by the size of the library and was, hopefully, 'sold' on the choice of study spaces. According to pre-arrival surveys of incoming UEL students' learning experiences prior to university, the wandering student was not an exception.

Curious about how UK universities pitch libraries in their online marketing information for prospective undergraduate students, I reviewed the websites of 20 UK institutions: 10 research-intensives and 10 modern universities. I selected the institutions from the *Times Higher University World Rankings 2024* list, roughly in sequential order (Times Higher Education, 2024).

Unsurprisingly, university libraries were showcased in the marketing materials on all university sites reviewed, although some were foregrounded more than others. Library information appeared under headings like 'Student Life', 'Facilities', 'Academic Support', or 'Campus Life'. EAB, which provides insights for the secondary to higher education sectors, notes that prospective students are less interested in university-created website 'sales' content and prefer first-person accounts from other students (Cousar, 2023). I noted evidence of this approach on some sites that featured 'a day in the life' of a student via a vlog or a student blog about campus life and good places to study. Of course, there were pictures of students reading books in libraries or working in modern study spaces. Libraries open 24/7 were also key 'selling points' for some institutions. Considering the ever-increasing cost of living, particularly for students, minimising heating costs by studying in the library must be a plus!

Where current institutional strategies were accessible, libraries were overtly mentioned in a few university strategies and in a couple of enabling estate strategies. Investment in 'physical spaces', 'learning spaces' and 'study spaces' was often mentioned in the estate strategies viewed. Some of these spaces may well be within or part of library spaces. Some university and estate strategies were due for refresh, with consultation underway. Where new libraries have been built or major refurbishment has been undertaken, these libraries may not be due for further investment in the current investment cycle.

As advised in the student guides, good library facilities are an important consideration when students are choosing universities. University and estates strategies need to evidence investment in libraries and other facilities to help to 'sell' the university. Library leaders are well positioned to inform institutional strategies to develop facilities that meet the needs of prospective students. Like my son's mates, many students may not appreciate the 'value' of the library until they actually need it.

Existing students

Having 'sold' a university experience complete with high-quality facilities to attract students, university leaders must maintain or enhance these to retain students. This means making good on investment promises, responding to student feedback on their experiences of using facilities such as libraries and involving students, academics and service leaders – key stakeholders – in institutional decision making. As noted earlier, the *Student Room Uni Guide* recommends that prospective students look at satisfaction scores in surveys such as the NSS (Gardner, 2023). The responses on the NSS are a useful tool for gaining some insights into student experiences of the university 'product' so that it can be enhanced ahead of the next 'sale' to incoming cohorts. In NSS 2023, question 20 asked students to provide a positivity rating on a Likert scale (e.g., agree to disagree) for the statement: 'How well have library resources (e.g., books, online services, and learning spaces) supported your learning?' The institutions reviewed all received satisfaction ratings of 88–97%. So, the libraries appear to be doing something right!

As the NSS provides little detail about what is going right or wrong, it needs to be triangulated with other internal metrics such as module evaluation questionnaires, quality reviews, course committee feedback and/or student forums. Once issues are raised, good customer service practice such as that defined in the Customer Services Excellence (CSE) standard needs to be applied. The CSE is a UK government standard for continuous improvement in customer service delivery (Cabinet Office, 2024). The standard provides guidelines on delivering consistently outstanding customer service and managing customer expectations through clear and timely communication. Poor customer service can lead to disgruntled students and bad publicity on social media with international reach that can adversely affect the university brand.

To illustrate, many libraries, particularly those in metropolitan areas like London, are susceptible to mice. At one library that I led, we found evidence of mice shredding books to create nests. The team embarked on a campaign to discourage students from eating in the library so as to effectively 'starve' the mice so that they would go elsewhere. In response, some students mounted a 'cruelty to mice' counter campaign on social media. Although the student campaign was in jest, broadcasting that the library had a mice problem was not good publicity for the institution. The library team had to rethink the campaign.

In the AdvanceHE/HEPI (UK) student academic experience report in 2021, 28% of respondents identified course facilities/resources as poor value, and 12% identified university buildings and campus as such. Tuition fees and contact hours scored worst as poor value, at 59% and 47%, respectively (Neves and Hewitt, 2021). Students' responses in the 2021 report were heavily influenced by their experiences during the COVID-19 pandemic restrictions, e.g., isolation due to movement restrictions and the rapid pivot to online delivery. Although course resources/facilities remained in the top ten concerns of poor value in 2023, the proportion of respondents with this concern decreased to 19% (Neves and Stephenson, 2023). It should be noted that students in the research were choosing from a predefined list of options for poor value; however, library, university and estates and facilities leaders must take note of these findings and consider the implications for their institutions.

The Office for Students (OfS) is the regulatory body which sets conditions for registration for English higher education institutions (HEI). The condition about resources, support and student engagement (B2) requires that: 'each cohort of students registered on each higher education course receives resources and support which are sufficient for the purpose of ensuring: (i) a high-quality academic experience for those students. . .' (Office for Students, 2022). Library resources such as books and journals can be in physical or electronic version, but *resources* also include computers to access e-content and study spaces for students to work. So, the library is integral to enabling the institution to meet the OfS B2 condition of registration. Admittedly, meeting these conditions is more about compliance than 'selling' the university; however, any hint of non-compliance could be flagged in social and mainstream media by higher education (HE) wonks, again adversely impacting on the university's brand.

Collections, partnerships and philanthropy

Academic libraries with collections of local, national and/or international significance can attract high-quality researchers, scholars and research funding. Research-intensive institutions, particularly, like those in the top of the THE league table discussed earlier, are expected by their researchers to negotiate affordable deals that enable read and publish access to high-impact journals. Libraries with archive services are also important attractions for the institution and the wider community, which can have positive reputational impact.

For example, UEL holds the Refugee Council Archive (RCA), which documents the history of displaced people since World War 2. Held and managed within our Archives Services, the collection is consulted by internal and external researchers and augmented by stories from the local community, such as the oral history of British Ugandan Asians who resettled in the UK after their forced migration from Uganda. The RCA collection is also integral to embedding research-informed teaching in the university curriculum, educating undergraduate students in using primary resources for their work.

The UEL Archives Services successfully bid for an Archives Revealed Scoping Grant which enables the development, discovery and preservation of the RCA. Archives Revealed is a partnership programme between The National Archives, The Pilgrim Trust and the Wolfson Foundation, and is committed to making UK archives accessible. The award of the grant reinforced the national importance of the RCA and positively impacts on the reputation of the wider institution.

UEL also holds the British Olympic Association (BOA) archive, which includes correspondence, meeting minutes and materials relating to London's hosting of the Olympic Games in 1908, 1948 and 2012. Among the many uses of the BOA collection is the UEL Sport in Your Future programme, aimed at encouraging school children in East London into physical activity and sport. As part of the programme, the children are able to engage with BOA memorabilia, including lifting an Olympic torch! Perhaps some of those school children will become future UEL scholars or researchers.

Just as institutions embark on partnerships that align with their values and strategy, so must they give the same due consideration to accepting donations and gifts. Librarians are accustomed to well-meaning individuals donating collections to libraries. Before accepting these gifts, a member of the library team assesses the offering for alignment with the existing collection, the condition of the items, and whether the library has sufficient space to store those items. Institutions will make similar assessments about partnerships on a larger scale, alongside a risk assessment of reputational impact.

The decolonisation movement spearheaded by student activism has compelled institutions to critically assess their own legacy as well as that of their partners, and, where there was harm, to reckon with it and address it. In her article entitled 'Neo-colonial Philanthropy in the UK', Fozia Irfan characterises philanthropy as 'paternalistic' and with a 'historic context of empire-building, slavery, and colonialism' (Irfan, 2021). This sentiment has been evidenced in the Rhodes Must Fall campaign initiated by students in South Africa (Fairbanks, 2015) and subsequent campaigns that have led to statues of historical figures with links to slavery being removed and names of streets and buildings being changed. Some students may factor the ethics of an institution and its partners into their decision making about a university. Climate change, global conflicts, cost of living are all causes that are important to students who will challenge their institutions and their supply chain to take ethical stances.

Of course, having the right donor(s), aligned politically and strategically, can be beneficial to an institution. In the US, fundraising from alumni is common practice. I received requests for donations as soon as I graduated from undergraduate and graduate education. One university library in the US dedicated study rooms to previous graduating classes that donated to the library, e.g., Class of 1985. Other institutions have dedicated collections, reading rooms or entire buildings to major donors.

Havens in the storm

UEL aims to be the UK's best careers-focused institution. The library provides an enabling function in the delivery of this strategy, but it can be difficult to spotlight the important work of the library team around critical thinking – particularly in the age of artificial intelligence (AI) – and information literacy, which both support and transcend employability. However, this dynamic shifted for a time after March 2020.

Library buildings closed in March 2020 due to COVID-19 pandemic restrictions. However, by June 2020 colleagues and I were on campus planning how to safely reopen the library buildings to provide computers, study spaces and Wi-Fi for those students who had no, limited or unreliable access to these resources at home during lockdown. In preparation for reopening, I stockpiled antiseptic wipes, gloves, masks and other personal protective equipment to ensure that we had an adequate stock upon opening.

By July 2020, we reopened both libraries in line with government guidance on physical distancing, cleaning, ventilation, etc. Although student residence support teams, security and student support services continued to operate throughout restrictions, other university buildings remained closed. The libraries were the first of these university buildings to reopen to students, much to the delight of those without adequate resources or places to work during restrictions. The libraries were hailed as areas of best practice for safe service delivery and management of the return of staff to site. And the libraries were showcased in institutional promotional materials evidencing that the University was open for business.

UEL's pedagogy for teaching and learning evolved in alignment with government guidance and the libraries were integral to that delivery. In 2020–21, teaching was provided via 'dual delivery'. This was characterised by the institution as 'digitally connected, 24/7 learning environments' and 'synchronous and asynchronous delivery' (University of East London, 2020). In practice, it meant that students could attend lectures online or in person and access learning resources online at any time. Students began to use the libraries to watch online lectures on PCs or laptops, often without headphones and/or in large groups. The library team directed students to collaborative or group study zones to mitigate the impact of residual noise filtering into the quiet and silent study zones.

By 2021/22 as on-campus activities increased, the institution embarked on technology-enhanced active learning (TEAL). This was characterised by the University as 'immersive learning environments, online study tools, access to recorded lectures, personalised analytics' (University of East London, n.d.) The libraries, with their 24/7 opening hours during teaching and exam periods, continued to be the location for students to access their online resources and work collaboratively with their peers. We were able to increase the availability of technology-rich group study spaces and bookable study rooms in the libraries for students to engage with their studies.

The library as a key destination for study is evidenced in the 2023 digital experience survey by JISC (Joint Information Systems Committee; a UK digital, data and technology provider), with 79% of respondents identifying 'on campus: study spaces, libraries, lectures, labs' as locations for using technology (JISC, 2023). At UEL, the libraries are the largest providers of open access computing and study spaces. In the same JISC report, 29% of respondents identified library/learning resources staff as sources for help with digital skills and technology, while 61% looked to their peers for support (JISC Data Analytics, 2023). The availability of peer support workers, called 'Digital First Aiders' at UEL, offers a choice of support for students in person and online. So, whether in international crisis or business as usual, libraries are havens of support for university students and staff.

Not just part of the scenery

Have you ever noticed how shelves laden with erudite books are often the backgrounds in video interviews and webinars? Perhaps this is because, historically, the display of a library of books within one's home was a sign of intellect, wealth and prestige. As the Docklands Library overlooks the Royal Albert Docks in London, it is a popular 'set' location for the communications department and film students alike. It is great to see the libraries on the evening news, for example, as an academic is interviewed about their research or executive leaders discuss university initiatives. The story may not be *about* the library, but publicity about the spaces may pique the interest of a viewer to learn more about what UEL has to offer.

Carefully managed and monitored, student posts on social media can also be useful publicity for libraries. There is no shortage of TikTok videos of students and animals wandering around university libraries, providing informal, virtual tours of the spaces. As discussed earlier, prospective students are more interested in learning about universities from existing students than via polished university promotional materials. So, a vlog by a student using their favourite library space can tell a positive story. When the film *Barbie* was released in 2023, communications staff members created a video in which they donned pink and popped out of UEL library stacks espousing their excitement about the film's opening. It was a bit of fun, and the shots of the library looked great.

During the celebration of the 125th anniversary of UEL, we invited students to write stories, whether real or imagined, about their experiences in the libraries. Called *Between the Stacks: Encounters in University of East London Libraries* (UEL Libraries, 2023), the stories were also published on the library website, with teasers from the stories displayed on LCD screens and posters. The printed collection of stories is stored in the University archive for the next 125 years. One contribution in the collection was a poem intentionally generated using ChatGPT 4.0, an open AI tool. The plots of the students' stories were generally about romance, making friends and finding a sense of belonging.

At institutions where I have worked previously, student publications helped to promote the library as a place to meet friends. One publication had a 'spotted' section, where students would post anonymous messages about something or someone interesting that they spotted in university spaces like the library. Another publication identified a specific comfy space in the library as a great place to meet people. And the library was the location of a silent disco as a passive approach to a student protest. All these activities, if carefully managed, can create a buzz around libraries and, potentially, draw in those who have yet to explore the space. Moreover, if students did not value the spaces, they would not have engaged in these activities.

Conclusion

An executive leader (EL) at an institution where I worked previously once said to me, 'I don't understand what you do'. Cue the lead balloon drop! This comment was made after the EL had held drop-in sessions for university staff and students in the library. The team and I were keen to host the sessions, as we saw it as an opportunity to showcase the library and its work.

The library team promoted the sessions and encouraged students to take advantage of the opportunity to share their views directly with an EL. The EL held multiple drop-in sessions in the library and seemed to enjoy engaging with the library team. Yet, the EL felt that the role of the library was unclear!

As ever, I chastised myself for not adequately selling the value of the service to the EL. The fact that the library was well used and sometimes at capacity, did well in national satisfaction surveys and was in demand by external researchers seemed to count for little. I knew the importance of ELs understanding the role of the library so that investment in the building and services could be baked into university and estate strategies. However, internally, I was seething at the fact that I had to *sell* what I knew was a fundamental facility and service. Yes, all faculties, schools and services must make business cases for why their area requires investment more urgently than others, that sometimes library investment may not be top of the list of priorities. However, for an EL to be unconvinced of the role of libraries in providing students with the resources, skills and support to be successful academically, in employment and beyond was frustrating, to say the least. Had I been a more seasoned library leader, I perhaps would have conjured the trope of the cleaner working at NASA who said that he was putting a man on the moon. I would have said, 'I'm developing the next world leader!' Instead, I fantasised about closing the library to see whether the EL could figure out our role then. That was before COVID-19.

As much of the work of libraries is digital (e.g., online catalogue, e-resources, tools for self-paced learning), the pivot online during COVID-19 restrictions was less painful for libraries than for faculties and schools delivering courses online. However, the impact of the loss of access to the physical spaces was well publicised in the HE sector worldwide. Academic libraries in the UK were among the earliest academic buildings to reopen as restrictions eased, and universities eagerly cited them as evidence of campus reopening. By then I had moved on from my previous university, but wondered whether the EL understood the value of the library during the COVID-19 restrictions when buildings were closed, and students and staff could access services only online.

The 'perceived value' of the library to that EL was seemingly barely on the functional (lower) rung of Bain & Company Inc.'s 'Elements of Value Pyramid' (Almquist et al., 2016). However, during the COVID-19 restrictions, when students and staff were reliant on library spaces not only for access to resources but for community and connections with others during a frightening and uncertain time, I would like to believe that the value of the library for the EL progressed rapidly from functional (basic needs) to emotional (wellness), life-changing (belonging) and, possibly, social impact!

Having gained more experience and confidence as a library leader, I have more tools in my arsenal to develop business cases for funding to support library development. I am also clear that libraries, like all university assets, need investment to continue to attract and retain students. Although students like my son's mates may take a bit of time to find the library, it's there when they need it. So, if again an EL says that they don't know what I do, I will say, 'The same as you. Sell the university.'

Addendum: Institution sites reviewed

Note: all sites accessed 27–29 January 2024.
Anglia Ruskin University
  www.aru.ac.uk/our-prospectuses
  www.aru.ac.uk/about-us/governance/strategy-and-leadership
University of Birmingham
  www.birmingham.ac.uk/study/undergraduate/prospectus
  www.birmingham.ac.uk/university/our-strategy
Birmingham City University
  www.bcu.ac.uk/courses/prospectus
  www.bcu.ac.uk/about-us/bcu-2025
Bournemouth University
  www.bournemouth.ac.uk/undergraduate-prospectus
  www.bournemouth.ac.uk/about/bu2025-our-vision-values-strategic-plan
University of Bristol
  www.bristol.ac.uk/study/undergraduate/order-a-
  prospectus/?wbraid=CjoKCAiA4b2MBhB9EioA8txKzbzP0kNaLFuLwjii
  8lUkZEwVKjdROch51r6igsGw0G0sMT7BWBAaAtHo
  https://bristol.ac.uk/university/media/vision/university-strategy-
  2030.pdf
University of Cambridge
  www.undergraduate.study.cam.ac.uk/sites/www.undergraduate.
  study.cam.ac.uk/files/publications/uoc_2024_ugp.pdf
  www.em.admin.cam.ac.uk/reshaping-our-estate
De Montfort University
  www.dmu.ac.uk/study/courses/january-start/index.aspx
  www.dmu.ac.uk/empowering-university/index.aspx
University of East London
  https://issuu.com/universityofeastlondon/docs/ug24
  https://uel.ac.uk/about/vision-2028
The University of Edinburgh
  www.ed.ac.uk/studying/undergraduate
  www.ed.ac.uk/sites/default/files/atoms/files/estates_vision.pdf

University of Glasgow
www.gla.ac.uk/media/Media_939699_smxx.pdf
www.gla.ac.uk/explore/strategy
University of Greenwich
https://docs.gre.ac.uk/rep/communications-and-
recruitment/undergraduate-prospectus
https://docs.gre.ac.uk/__data/assets/pdf_file/0034/287953/uog-
strategy.pdf
https://docs.gre.ac.uk/rep/ef/university-of-greenwich-estate-strategy-to-
2030
University of Hertfordshire
www.herts.ac.uk/study/our-prospectuses
www.herts.ac.uk/about-us/our-leadership-strategy-and-plans/our-
strategy-vision-and-culture
www.herts.ac.uk/__data/assets/pdf_file/0019/321472/0292-MCW-00-
XX-RP-A-00001-S0-P3_2030-Estates-Vision-Final.pdf
University of Huddersfield
https://issuu.com/universityofhuddersfield/docs/huddersfield_uni_
undergraduate_prospectus_2324
www.hud.ac.uk/news/staff/2022/april/university-strategy-map
https://staff.hud.ac.uk/estates/strategicestateplanning
Imperial College London
www.imperial.ac.uk/study/request-info
www.imperial.ac.uk/strategy
www.imperial.ac.uk/study/request-info
www.imperial.ac.uk/strategy
King's College London
www.kcl.ac.uk/study/undergraduate/prospectus
www.kcl.ac.uk/about/strategy
The London School of Economics and Political Science
www.lse.ac.uk/study-at-lse/meet-visit-and-discover-LSE/experience-
lse/brochures
www.lse.ac.uk/2030
The University of Manchester
www.manchester.ac.uk/study/undergraduate/prospectus
www.manchester.ac.uk/discover/vision
Middlesex University
www.mdx.ac.uk/study-with-us/undergraduate/order-a-prospectus-ug
www.mdx.ac.uk/about-us/our-strategy-to-2031
University of Oxford
www.ox.ac.uk/digital-prospectus

https://staff.admin.ox.ac.uk/article/developing-plans-for-the-future-of-the-university-estate
University of Portsmouth
www.port.ac.uk/about-us/publications
www.port.ac.uk/about-us/our-ambition/our-strategy
University College London
www.ucl.ac.uk/news/2023/mar/undergraduate-prospectus-2024-entry-now-available
www.ucl.ac.uk/strategic-plan-2022-27/supporting-strategies/ucl-estates-strategy-2022-27
University of Warwick
https://warwick.ac.uk/study/undergraduate
https://warwick.ac.uk/about/strategy

References

Almquist, E., Senior, J. and Bloch, N. (2016) The Elements of Value, Harvard Business Review, September, https://hbr.org/2016/09/the-elements-of-value.
Cabinet Office (2024) Customer Service Excellence (CSE), www.customerserviceexcellence.uk.com.
Cousar, D. (2023) Prospects are Tired of your Advertisements. Organic Social Media can Change that, EAB, https://eab.com/resources/blog/adult-education-blog/prospects-tired-advertisements-organic-social-media-change/?
Fairbanks, E. (2015) The Birth of Rhodes Must Fall, *Guardian*, 18 November.
Gardner, A. (2023) Nine Things to Look for when Comparing University Courses, The Student Room Uni Guide, www.theuniguide.co.uk/advice/choosing-a-course/top-things-to-look-for-when-comparing-uni-courses.
Irfan, F. (2021) Neo-Colonial Philanthropy in the UK, Journal of Philanthropy and Marketing, **28** (4), e1726, https://onlinelibrary.wiley.com/doi/10.1002/nvsm.1726.
JISC Data Analytics (2023) Student Digital Experience Insights Survey 2022/23, JISC.
Mosse, T. (2024) A Student's Guide to Choosing the Right UK University, Complete University Guide, www.thecompleteuniversityguide.co.uk/student-advice/where-to-study/student-guide-to-choosing-right-uni.
National Literacy Trust (2021) The Future of Primary School Libraries, https://literacytrust.org.uk/research-services/research-reports/the-future-of-primary-school-libraries.

Neves, J. and Hewitt, R. (2021) Student Academic Experience Survey 2021, AdvanceHE/HEPI.

Neves, J. and Stephenson, R. (2023) Student Academic Experience Survey 2023, AdvanceHE/HEPI.

Office for Students (2022) Registration with the OfS, www.officeforstudents.org.uk/advice-and-guidance/regulation/registration-with-the-ofs-a-guide/conditions-of-registration.

Park, J. (2023) School Library Provision Suffers from 'Inequality of Access', Research Finds, Twinkl Digest Education News, 9 March, www.twinkl.co.uk/news/school-library-provision-suffers-from-inequality-of-access-research-finds.

Smith, S. (2023) 20 Things to Compare when Looking at Unis, What Uni? www.whatuni.com/advice/choosing-a-uni/20-things-to-compare-when-looking-at-unis/67613.

Times Higher Education (2024) World University Rankings, www.timeshighereducation.com/world-university-rankings/2024/world-ranking.

UEL Libraries (2023) Between the Stacks: Encounters in University East London Libraries.

University of East London (2020) UEL Dual Delivery Education Framework (2020–21), UEL Intranet.

University of East London (n.d.) Technology Enhanced Active Learning, https://uelac.sharepoint.com/sites/home/SitePages/Technology-Enhanced-Active-Learning-(TEAL).aspx.

6

The Library Through a Workplace Lens: A Conversation with Neil Everitt

Regina Everitt: Let's start with your experience of using academic libraries.

Neil Everitt: As a mature student at Birkbeck, University of London, I used the library spaces as the transition from work to study, to take time to breathe, to catch up, before evening lectures. This (precious) 45 minutes or so, three times a week, gave me the opportunity to have some 'me time', important to an introvert, and replenish my energy reserves before the evening lectures.

The library also created a connection with the University 'space'. This may have been replaced by other spaces such as the Students' Union if I had been studying full time perhaps – but the library was an important element of how I remember my Birkbeck experience. Another major element of that experience was the support provided to utilise the resources available through the library and aid my transition into academic study.

Later, studying at Cranfield University, the space in and around the library was used to collaborate as part of small study teams, as part of a larger cohort of students, designed to replicate the way teams operate in organisations. The study teams provided support to their members by dividing the workload, and working together on projects and case studies, and created natural competition between the study teams. The teams were given free rein to utilise the variety of spaces available at the University, but speed was needed to bag the most appropriate space for the task, to avoid five tired and over-caffeinated individuals huddling around a single laptop screen as a spreadsheet was analysed or last-minute tweaks to a presentation were agreed. On reflection, I wonder if the freedom to use a range of spaces was designed into the course to provide a challenge to everyone on the course to better understand the way they preferred to learn and work, complete a range of different work activities and assess the optimal space to achieve this.

RE: Turning to workplace and facilities management, what is the purpose of IWFM?

NE: When I joined the Institute of Workplace and Facilities Management (IWFM) back in 2009, I must admit I knew little about professional bodies or facilities management (FM) but I thought it would make an interesting change after years of working for a large multinational mining company. My interest in property and facilities management was piqued while undertaking a volunteer procurement project for a local charity that provided community space and outreach. It took a while to understand the many and varied tasks and responsibilities facilities managers were taking on – 'administration' in the language of my previous employer – as well as elements needed to codify such a wide-ranging and newly emerging profession. But over time many colleagues and member volunteers helped me to understand the mechanics of the profession, the impact it can have on enabling organisations to function effectively and the role professional bodies play.

The IWFM formed in 1993 as the British Institute of Facilities Management (BIFM) after merging the Association of Facilities Managers with the Institute of Facilities Management to create a single UK-based membership body.

Although IWFM's purpose has been to 'advance the profession', the FM function was still often seen by business leaders as a cost centre, with 'support services' often delivered by outsourced suppliers or partners.

But in 2016 the Stoddart Review (2016) was published, which argued that the profession was well placed to adopt a 'super-connector' role in bringing together the sometimes disparate functions of corporate real estate, facilities management, IT (information technology) and HR (human resources) to create 'the workplace advantage' for organisations and increase productivity.

Although productivity means different things to different organisations, the debate had previously ignored the workplace. This influential report quantified the significant contribution a well-designed workplace can make to productivity.

In November 2018, the BIFM formally changed its name to the Institute of Workplace and Facilities Management or IWFM, thus repositioning FM as a value creator with even greater potential to enable business success.

IWFM's stated vision is a future 'Where every workplace delivers' (IWFM, 2024a), and recognition of the critical nature of the profession in informing strategy, providing solutions and enabling outcomes.

As a long-standing employee of IWFM, I am sometimes asked why do we focus on workplaces, meaning office spaces, and ignore FM in other sectors, for example education? My response is that workplace and facilities management professionals can add most value when they are able to influence the key measures of productivity of an organisation, like universities and libraries, be it staff satisfaction, health and well-being in the knowledge economy or student and patient outcomes in education and health, rather than solely managing the physical space.

RE: Why is it important to foreground 'workplace' in the organisation's title?

NE: Historically, the FM function within many organisations was seen as providing a wide range of services such as cleaning, security and building maintenance; these services were often outsourced and procured at 'best value', and in the background, as long as they didn't negatively impact on the organisations' 'core-business'. In some organisations facilities managers also took responsibility for health and safety, risk, business continuity, procurement, sustainability, space planning, energy, property and asset management.

Over more recent years the FM community has worked through national standards agencies to develop a range of FM standards and a single International Organization for Standardization (ISO) definition of FM as the 'organizational function which integrates people, place and process within the built environment with the purpose of improving the quality of life of people and the productivity of the core business' (ISO, 2024).

This definition acknowledges the integration role which FM plays and its impact on the people and productivity of organisations.

But can the profession go beyond the built environment and jointly influence FM, IT, HR and other colleagues such as library professionals to achieve optimal performance between people, technology and workspace? In the case of universities, how can the profession influence institutional strategy and be a critical delivery partner to enable the best possible student outcomes?

Property often represents the second largest proportion of any organisation's costs (after people), so when organisations bring people together in space which is costing money there must be a value to doing so, be it through making connections or engendering joint purpose or enhancing the culture. The pandemic challenged the way organisations work, as well as the way people want to work (Oldman, 2023).

The challenge for workplace professionals is how best to interconnect between specialisms to optimise business performance, to empower work wherever it takes place and to make workplaces productive.

Although the Stoddart Review provided case studies and data, and there exist methodologies to measure and benchmark workplace experience, e.g., the Leesman Index, a single, direct causal link to the productivity of an organisation remains elusive.

Workplace expert Neil Usher (2018) argues that workplace productivity can be both objective (i.e., measurable) and subjective, for example how the user feels. He questions whether a clear return on investment is needed if we assume that providing better facilities contributes to better work by people, as well as being the right thing to do.

Usher builds on work created by Frank Duffy to create a framework to answer 'why' workplace is critical and provide a 'staircase pitch' to make the case for change to workplaces (Duffy, 2009). Usher (2018) builds on Duffy's 3-Es – efficiency, effectiveness and expression – and has added environment, ether and energy.

The need for *efficiency* is often the driver for workplace change as leases come to an end or additional study spaces are needed. This can be objectively measured through cost efficiency (cost per sq. ft/metre or cost per person in a defined space), and space efficiency (occupation density and space utilisation). Usher points out that in non-asset-based organisations approximately 85% of the operational cost base is people, with property 10% and IT 5%. He says that 70% of the property costs can be non-discretionary such as rent, service charges, etc. He highlights that the impact of the 30% discretionary spend, as work ceases to be conducted in a single location, can often be overlooked in the drive for efficiency (Usher, 2018).

The *effectiveness* of a space refers to the way the space is configured to enable work, for example, collaboration or lone working, the correct technology and systems, as well as amenities. Usher (2018) highlights the importance of considering the balance between efficiency and effectiveness and alignment with the organisation's objectives. Is the cost of the workplace versus the value to the workforce supporting or detracting from the organisation's ability to deliver its strategy?

The *expression* of space questions whether it aligns with an organisation's brand and enables individuals to be themselves while creating a coherent association and commitment from staff and users of the space to the organisation.

The importance of *environment* is growing as organisations consider not just what they do but how they do it. Organisations are increasingly committing to becoming net zero and requiring Energy Performance Certificate (EPC) rating. They are also seeking benchmarking and accreditation from schemes such as BREEAM (Building Research Establishment Assessment Methodology) In-Use standard to improve asset performance (BRE, 2024), green building rating system Leadership in Energy and Environmental Design (LEED) (USGBC, 2024), and supporting the delivery of spaces to enhance health and well-being by adhering to the WELL standard (IWBI, 2024).

Usher (2018) points out that *ether* – the reviews, feedback and way an organisation is viewed, both online and in person – is becoming increasingly important, and an area where workplace can contribute to the overall perception of an organisation.

The final of the six elements to consider is *energy*, or the impact of the space(s) where work takes place on the well-being of the users. Does it sap or enhance the energy of the user?

All six elements are arguably as relevant in a university campus context as in an office building.

RE: Library teams are key stakeholders for FM practitioners. How does your organisation help facilities managers to develop the relevant skills to effectively support their customers?

NE: If the workplace and FM professional is to be seen as a critical delivery partner, a trusted consultant, able to deliver business outcomes and support productivity, a deep understanding of what a range of stakeholders need and how to effectively engage them is a critical success factor. IWFM includes stakeholder relationships as part of its 'Professional Standards' competency framework.

The Association for Project Management defines stakeholder engagement as: the systematic identification, analysis, planning and implementation of actions designed to influence stakeholders (APM, 2024). The consultancy firm AccountAbility published a stakeholder engagement strategy standard which provides a framework and process to develop a stakeholder engagement strategy (AccountAbility, 2015).

The Institute of Chartered Accountants in England and Wales (ICAEW, 2024) argues that stakeholder engagement has several key benefits, including being able to better identify emerging issues and improve decision making, support a more robust approach to strategic planning and provide different perspectives on key issues and risks.

ICAEW (2024) also argue that there are several key principles of effective stakeholder engagement: listening, not just transmitting messages, understanding the reciprocal nature of relationships, as well as showing a willingness to learn.

Developing an approach which incorporates all these principles is crucial for organisations to develop effective stakeholder engagement which can help to deliver improved organisational performance and outcomes. It is also important that stakeholder engagement is clearly scoped and integrated into strategic and operational plans, and activity and accountability agreed. It is crucial to ensure that there is commitment and integration of stakeholder management into the organisation's governance and decision making, strategy and operational plans. Equally important is to agree on the stakeholders to be engaged, the purpose of the engagement and the scope or extent of the engagement, so as to deliver the organisational outcomes needed. The process to agree which stakeholders to engage should include a range of perspectives in order to avoid a superficial view; for example are a range of diverse views being considered which could be challenging? Agreeing a clear purpose for the engagement should consider the alignment with the overall organisational and departmental strategies. The scope and activities to deliver the engagement can then be agreed, along with clear accountability for delivery (AccountAbility, 2015).

The process recommended by AccountAbility (2015) is to plan, prepare, implement, and act, review and improve. The planning and preparation will involve agreeing the stakeholder groups and individual stakeholders and mapping. Often this considers influence and interest, but could also include other elements such as willingness to engage. The types of engagement should then be considered, how much, and the mode of communication – whether information sharing by website, e-mail, focus groups, advisory panels and joint projects are most appropriate. The engagement plan can then be created and should be supported with regular reviews of the stakeholders and activities.

For many organisations a formal approach to stakeholder engagement may be in place and delivering the outcomes desired. For others a less structured approach may be used. A challenge for organisations which the AccountAbillity approach exposes is the extent to which the organisation takes a consistent approach to stakeholder engagement in order that the governance, strategy and operational approach is in place to support the stakeholder engagement. Without consistency of approach, pockets of the organisation may implement different approaches, but will the outcomes be optimised for the organisation?

Most professionals seem to have an implicit understanding of stakeholder engagement, but a more structured approach can be valuable.

RE: Library leaders often need to manage changes to service delivery after an estates project handover. How can the professions work together to make this a smooth transition?

NE: To be able to deliver business outcomes, library and facilities management professionals need to be comfortable with, and able to orchestrate, change.

De Wit and Meyer (1998) contrast two quotes by the artist Pablo Picasso and the author of Aesop's Fables. Picasso said that 'Every act of creation is first of all an act of destruction', while the motto of the Aesop's fable of The Hare and the Tortoise is 'Slow and steady wins the race'.

The two quotes show the dichotomy facing professionals accountable for delivering a service and the disruptive change projects which occur less frequently. The requirement to deliver evolutionary or continuous improvement to a service is approached differently to the revolutionary or discontinuous change to deliver a project.

Strategists De Wit and Meyer (1998) argue that successful continuous change is long term in orientation and that employees need to be committed to both continuous improvement and continuous learning, as advocated by Peter Senge (Senge, 1990). They argue that this long-term orientation is like successful marathon runners, who can sustain their efforts for long periods, versus sprinters, who can move more quickly but are not able to sustain their efforts for the marathon.

De Wit and Meyer (1998) also argue that in most organisations there is a resistance to change, and therefore pressure is needed – abrupt and dramatic. But periods of stability are required to create structured communication, co-ordination, standards and routines. Therefore this type of change is not gradual but episodic.

Defining the type of change is largely a factor of the magnitude of change – moderate and piecemeal versus radical and dramatic – and the pace of change – gradual and constant versus abrupt and intermittent. Continuous change requires organisational or teamwide buy-in and commitment to achieving small improvements over time. Discontinuous change, abrupt and dramatic, is often initiated by senior management and assisted by consultants.

According to De Wit and Meyer (1998), change is often described by reference to established models such as the Kubler-Ross' 'grieving curve' (phases of shock, denial, frustration, depression, experimentation, acceptance and integration), Lewin's three-stages (unfreeze, change, refreeze) and Kotter's eight-step guide.

Neil Usher (2018) argues that change within a workplace setting is often not a sequential or linear journey and offers a framework to assist as change is enacted. He counsels that there is a need for participants in the change to be able to say three things to create a connection and effective participation in the change: firstly, they can say 'I know' – they are aware of what is happening and why; secondly, they can say 'I feel' – they have an emotional connection and are engaged; thirdly, they can say 'I will do' – they are involved and committed to taking action.

In a university setting, the estates project handover would seem to be particularly important to achieving the 'episodic' change envisaged, as well as the continuous service delivery improvement expected.

RE: How has the FM profession evolved over time, in your view?

NE: As the workplace and facilities management profession has developed, the understanding of the core competences required has evolved, has become more defined, and its critical and value adding role is better understood.

All other established professions have a way to assess a practitioner's knowledge, skills and competence, be it passing an assessment, relevant experience or mandating continuing professional development. There now exists a range of certifications available to workplace and facilities management professionals. Alongside a range of regulated qualifications and professional membership pathway, IWFM has also developed, with industry, a competency framework, Professional Standards, which provides competency standards at five levels from support to strategic across ten competency areas (IWFM, 2024b).

The profession offers opportunities to progress, and it is not unusual to see practitioners progressing from lower-level roles to become director of estates or director of workplace. It is also common for people to come into the profession from other areas, for example engineering, property or hospitality, even libraries, and build on their existing knowledge and skills, and progress.

The range of roles within the profession presents a fantastic opportunity for practitioners to take on new challenges, but also presents a challenge when trying to codify the competences required for specific roles.

How practitioners identify themselves as workplace and facilities management professionals can be impacted on by factors such as the sector they work in, the organisation they work for, the role they have or who they report to. IWFM conducts an annual Market Outlook survey, with one of the questions asking the person if they view their work as 'managing workspaces' or 'enabling work wherever it happens'. Since 2020 the proportion of respondents identifying as 'managing workspaces' has hovered just below 50%, with 'enabling work' consistently around 40% (IWFM, 2023a). The numbers may have been impacted by the changing work patterns brought on by COVID-19, but there remains a clear split in terms of identity.

There are factors which are impacting the profession and what it is being asked to take responsibility for, such as sustainability and technology. Sustainability is becoming increasingly important for organisations, with CO_2 emissions coming from the built environment, and the supply chain emissions (scope 3) which often account for 70% of an organisation's emissions (IWFM, 2023b). However, the IWFM Sustainability Survey in 2023 found that 86% of respondents lacked the integrated comprehensive skills to deliver net zero aspirations, 69% lacked the comprehensive baseline and ongoing data and 43% lacked clear net zero targets. Similarly, 16% of respondents felt their organisation had well-integrated digital technology, 52% were not able to combine data from different sources and 63% reported the high upfront costs of installing technologies as the biggest barrier to better outcomes (IWFM, 2023b).

But as workplace and facilities management professionals are asked to develop competence across a range of business disciplines what should they be truly responsible for, and how do they connect, from an expertise in buildings, with colleagues with deep expertise in human resources or IT? Being seen as a critical delivery partner, a trusted consultant, able to deliver business outcomes and support productivity would seem to be key.

At a recent event, senior business leaders in workplace and facilities management were asked what is the key skill that they have needed to be successful within their careers; one of the answers was influencing. This might be by improving user experience by reinvesting in the design of library spaces while delivering the finance director's request to cut costs, implementing ideas to improve well-being of staff to support HR colleagues, or finding new ways to work with suppliers to reduce food waste.

RE: Libraries and the university sector have experienced changes in use and operations since the COVID-19 pandemic. What are your observations of the FM profession since the pandemic?

NE: IWFM captures the sentiment of members about the facilities management market and factors impacting on the profession through a variety of research. The annual Market Outlook survey provides insight to how UK-based practitioners see the challenges and performance of the FM market, and other research such as the annual Sustainability survey captures performance and provides recommendations for the future.

The once-in-a-generation impact of COVID-19 on the way organisations operate is still in the process of working its way through many organisations' plans. The realisation that many workers, especially those traditionally office based, can work effectively from home was a shock, and organisations are taking a variety of approaches to managing this hybrid environment.

The research finding by Leesman that the average home supports work better than the average office, presents a challenge to the traditional organisational structure and processes, but highlights worker sentiment and the subconscious trade-offs made when considering the cost and time of commuting, and benefits of configuring your home workspace exactly as you want it, versus the collective benefits of getting people together (Oldman, 2023).

Oldman (2023) highlights that senior leaders are asking why is the space needed if they have operated as an organisation without it for over two years during COVID? He argues that the debate should not be one of home versus office, but rather home plus office, but this requires organisations to adopt a new hybrid culture and social contract to better enable employees to work effectively, wherever that is. He advocates for traditional property professionals to be supplemented by new skills in hospitality, event planning and communication, to deliver this new vision.

Oldman (2023) also cites Leesman research where 20% of senior property professionals surveyed said their organisations are looking at considerable reductions (25–50%) in real estate footprint, and 39% of respondents cited a minor (less than 25%) reduction. In addition to space reduction, he also references where value engineering is being considered, but counsels against engineering-out things which are important to people using the space. Can the space facilitate informal social interaction or unplanned meetings, create visibility and connection and nourish the organisation's culture? How can organisations navigate the tension between providing all individuals the ability to define their own workplaces, and creating a 'me' culture rather than an organisational culture, and how to manage employees' personal preferences versus collective benefit when making these decisions?

Oldman (2023) argues that the property supply chain generally has contracts with clear deliverables and penalties – and argues that this acts as a barrier to innovation in providing organisations with solutions needed in this new environment. Oldman (2023) proposes that in order to respond effectively organisations need to understand answers to a few key questions.

One: do you understand what your employees need in order to work effectively? Are the tasks being undertaken well defined and is the space configured to best support this? Does the space enhance productivity, engender pride and sense of community? Oldman (2023) cites previous Leesman research that individual 'focused work, desk-based' is the most influential component in the sense of experience and creates an environment of feeling supported. It may well be that the home environment is the better environment to support this – for example the challenge of managing noise levels in an office – while the office can better support collaborative activity, although he counsels that the number of people in organisations with collaborative roles is often overestimated.

So clear, understanding is needed about the activities of roles in the organisation, the number of people in highly collaborative versus highly individual roles and the infrastructure required to fulfil these activities.

Two: understand the space available to employees at home. This is often overlooked, but Leesman research shows that young employees are generally not set up as well to work at home as more senior colleagues, and, alongside other motivating factors such as desire to learn and showcase talent, have a greater inclination to return to the office (Oldman, 2023). The question for many organisations is: who takes responsibility for gaining this insight? Is it the property teams; HR, who could be looking at it through a well-being prism; or IT, who provide significant support for hybrid workers?

Three: comparison with pre-pandemic environment. Workers historically considered costs associated with work, for example commuting, lunch, work socialising, as a cost of living. Oldman (2023) argues that this perception has changed now to a 'cost of working', where calls to return to the office will be traded off against the costs by workers. So, the perceived cost of being in an organisational space needs to be addressed by creating an environment where workers see the benefit of being there. He also argues for the need to measure how satisfied people are, with existing spaces to enable them to be effective and for the amount of time they spend there to be verified.

There is also a growing realisation that buildings need to be designed to welcome everyone, regardless of their characteristics or identity. Inclusive design considers factors which create effort and separation, and enables everyone to participate equally and independently. The Inclusive Design Overlay to RIBA (Royal Institute of British Architects) Plan of Work was developed by a variety of built-environment professions to support inclusive design and to equip and empower built-environment professionals with the knowledge to embed inclusive design into project delivery across all stages of the RIBA Plan of Work (RIBA, 2020).

In many organisations the accountability for optimising the working spaces, the IT infrastructure and the HR policies within the organisation's physical space is clear, but is there clarity when considering the employee's home or off-site working set-up? In a university setting, the interplay between the estates, libraries, student services and housing would seem to be key to providing the student the best possible environment to succeed.

RE: And how do you see the future of FM?

NE: The workplace and facilities management profession is evolving and responding to the changing environment impacting on the way that organisations operate. COVID-19 forced organisations to adapt quickly to continue to operate in a way unimaginable before March 2020. Each organisation is taking a different approach to how it operates going forward.

The profession is also being challenged to stay up to date with changes in legislation, including building safety (IWFM, 2024c), to provide solutions to net zero and sustainability, support health and well-being of employees and adopt opportunities presented by rapid development of data and technology. It is also being asked to provide the hospitality skills to attract employees back into the workplace, lead change and influence colleagues and the direction of organisations.

All of this will impact on the knowledge, skills and competence required within the profession.

Key questions for the workplace and facilities management profession are how it attracts, retains and develops its people. There are often-quoted examples of people falling into the profession, and evidence that skills and knowledge is being lost as established professionals retire. Workplace and facilities management has a heritage of pioneering women making a significant impact and progressing in the profession. Making the profession attractive, providing a variety of pathways in and options to develop and attain recognition are all crucial.

The UK Government Property Function published its FM strategy 2022–2030 to support the Government Property Strategy commitment 'to reshape the public estate, making it smaller, better, and greener, and able to support the transformation of places and services'.' A key element of the strategy is to have the FM professionals equipped with effective skills and capabilities, with the goal of having 90% of FM, workplace and maintenance senior practitioners and leaders accredited or working towards accreditation with an approved property professional body by 2030 (UK Government Property Function, 2022).

The Young Foundation report, *Beyond Buzzwords*, documented the experiences of surveyed members from 12 professional bodies, including IWFM, to investigate the state of equality, diversity and inclusion (EDI) initiatives today. Although the report highlighted the social and economic benefits that EDI can bring, it noted substantial barriers to progress. The report also highlighted the crucial role professional bodies can play in bringing about structural change to professions (Young Foundation, 2024).

The FM-specific findings made uncomfortable reading and evidenced the dangers of not acting, exacerbating an existing skills issue. The experiences of IWFM members in the report indicated that people in FM experience more severe discrimination and exclusion. More facilities managers change jobs, take career breaks, choose self-employment, experience mental health issues and turn down professional opportunities. They are more likely to exit FM because of issues related to EDI (IWFM, 2024d). The report also found that within marginalised groups, professionals disagree on the state of EDI progress, at best hampering progression. In an updated statement IWFM (2024d) committed to:

- putting EDI at the heart of professional life through updated codes of ethics/conduct, reviewing professional standards and reframing EDI as non-negotiable;
- foregrounding EDI in upskilling and reskilling, including the accreditation based on core competencies around EDI;
- creating opportunities for professionals to shape EDI in their organisation, such as forming working groups and building accountability through feedback and communication;
- ensuring all strategies, policies, procedures and practices are approached through an EDI lens, continuously monitoring progress.

Creating the conditions for the profession to be attractive and sustainable for people with different characteristics will be crucial. As a service profession, how is it possible to anticipate and respond to the wide variety of needs of your customers if the variety of people and views are not represented at senior levels of the profession?

References

AccountAbility (2015) AA1000 Stakeholder Engagement Strategy, www.accountability.org/standards/aa1000-stakeholder-engagement-standard.

APM (Association for Project Management) (2024) Stakeholder Engagement, www.apm.org.uk/resources/find-a-resource/stakeholder-engagement.

BRE (2024) BREEAM In-Use Standard, https://breeam.com/standards/in-use.

De Wit, R. and Meyer, R. (1998) *Strategy – Process, Content, Context*, Thomson Learning.

Duffy, F. (2009) Building Appraisal: A Personal View, *Journal of Building Appraisal*, 4 (3), 149–56.

ICAEW (Institute of Chartered Accountants in England and Wales) (2024) Stakeholder Mapping and Engagement, www.icaew.com/technical/corporate-governance/new-boardroom-agenda/guide-to-stakeholder-mapping-and-engagement.

ISO (2024) Definition of FM, www.iso.org/standard/82405.html.

IWBI (International WELL Building Institute) (2024) WELL Standard, www.wellcertified.com.

IWFM (2023a) Market Outlook Survey, www.iwfm.org.uk/resource/market-outlook-survey-report-2023.html?parentId=4450579B-41B1-452B-988514 09E1AA7B2C.

IWFM (2023b) Sustainability Survey,
www.iwfm.org.uk/resource/sustainability-survey-2023.html.

IWFM (2024a) IWFM's Vision, www.iwfm.org.uk/about.html.

IWFM (2024b) Professional Standards,
www.iwfm.org.uk/about/the-professional-standards.html.

IWFM (2024c) Fire Safety Management Good Practice Guide,
www.iwfm.org.uk/resource/fire-safety-
management.html?parentId=4450579B-41B1-452B-98851409E1AA7B2C.

IWFM (2024d) EDI Public Statement, www.iwfm.org.uk/resource/why-
iwfm-is-boosting-its-edi-commitment-and-what-it-means-for-the-lynchpin-
profession.html?parentId=8CBD03AD-C979-4553-
AB9AAA1F0AB1081A.

Leesman Index (2024) www.leesmanindex.com.

Oldman, T. (2023) *Why Workplace? A Leader's Guide to the Post-pandemic
Workplace*, Leesman Ltd.

RIBA (Royal Institute of British Architects) (2020) Inclusive Design Overlay
to the RIBA Plan of Work,
www.architecture.com/knowledge-and-resources/resources-landing-
page/inclusive-design-overlay-to-riba-plan-of-work.

Senge, P. (1990) *The Fifth Discipline: The Art and Practice of The Learning
Organization*, Random House.

Stoddart Review (2016) www.iwfm.org.uk/resource/the-stoddart-review-the-
workplace-advantage.html, Raconteur Custom Publishing.

UK Government Property Function (2022) *Facilities Management Strategy
2022–2030*,
https://assets.publishing.service.gov.uk/media/6364d68ee90e0734627b9ca
e/GPS-Facilities-Management.pdf.

USGBC (US Green Building Council) (2024) LEED Rating System,
www.usgbc.org/leed.

Usher, N. (2018) *The Elemental Workplace*, LID Publishing Ltd.

The Young Foundation (2024) Beyond Buzzwords: Embedding a Systemic
Approach to EDI across the UK's Professions,
www.youngfoundation.org/our-work/publications/beyond-buzzwords.

Part 2 Landings

7

Repurposing Library Study Space to Create a Family Study Room: A Case Study at University of Bradford

Alison Lahlafi

Introduction

The University of Bradford places strategic priority on embedding equality, diversity and inclusion (EDI) in all it does, as evidenced by the University frequently leading the sector in social inclusion and mobility rankings (HEPI, 2023). As Bradford's vice-chancellor stated, 'At Bradford, the principle of equality of opportunity is at the heart of who we are, what we do, how and why we do it,' (BBC, 2023). The University's 'Making our Diversity Count: Equality, Diversity and Inclusion Strategy 2020–25' (University of Bradford, 2020) puts emphasis on creating and promoting an inclusive working and learning environment at the University. The University of Bradford's J. B. Priestley Library is one of the key learning spaces within the University, and the library's strategy aligns with these university goals, voicing a strong commitment to providing a truly inclusive, safe and supportive learning environment for all library users.

Reviewing the inclusivity of library study spaces for our users

At the end of 2021, as part of a University of Bradford library staff reading and discussion group session, library staff discussed the article 'Meeting the Needs of Parents and Carers within Library Services: Responding to Student Voices at the University of East London' (Clover, 2017). This article talked about how the library at the University of East London had been investigating how it could be more responsive in meeting the needs of students who are parents/carers of young children. It included results from a student survey through which parents overwhelmingly requested a separate dedicated area to be set up, preferably encompassing activities for children. It also acknowledged that some university libraries in the United States (US) have created specific spaces for students with their children, although this solution was stated as not practicable in the space available to the library at the University of East London.

In early 2022, as part of work undertaken by the University of Bradford library team to maintain its Customer Services Excellence accreditation, the library team reviewed how inclusive and supportive current library spaces were for the range of students, staff and external users using them. The team used customer segmentation to help explore and understand the characteristics of Bradford's current and potential customer groups. This work highlighted a rise in the number of students seen around the library with small children. The library team were already aware of many students juggling studies with care for young children (defined here as under 12 years of age), and student parent/carers sometimes bringing young children to the library with them. Library staff referenced children being seen more across the University in café areas, running around the main library floor and sitting with parents/carers in the soft seating area of the library's Calm Space; babies and small children being brought to student appointments with subject librarians; and, on one occasion, library staff offering library office space for privacy to a breastfeeding student. Looking into this further, it was found that a recent increase in international student numbers at the University was also associated with a large percentage of these students joining the University with dependents. The Clover article, coupled with the library space review, cemented the library team's decision to further explore how the library might develop a more supportive and inclusive environment for our student parents/carers.

The library team decided to include university staff within the scope of the development of library family-friendly space. Both university staff and students are users of the library, and although our initial idea had just been focused on supporting student parent/carers, it was acknowledged that university staff also occasionally need to bring their children onto the campus. The library team therefore determined to try to improve the library experience for both university staff and student parents/carers with young children by repurposing a general library group study room as a dedicated bookable family study space. Although the library is used to rapidly adapting and repurposing spaces to meet the changing needs of users, the work on repurposing library study space to create a family study room was a surprisingly long journey, taking nearly two years to complete from initial concept to opening. It involved extremely close partnership work with the University's estates and health and safety teams, which sit within the overarching directorate of infrastructure, to successfully realise our vision.

The start of the journey

The journey started with further research and advocacy work to get buy-in from the University, as the library team quickly realised that the proposal to develop a dedicated space for families went against the University Children on Campus Policy. The policy in place in 2022, when the library started to look at developing a family study room, stated:

> University buildings are not designed with the attendance of children in mind, there are many hazards both in the layout of the buildings and in the equipment and machinery provided for teaching and other purposes […] The University will not allow the bringing of children onto University premises which is not part of a planned or permissible activity. Children should not be brought into the workplace due to failures in childcare provision.
>
> (University of Bradford, 2018)

In relation to the library, the policy also explicitly stated that students were permitted to come into the library with their children for only a brief visit, the example given being 'briefly attending the Library to return a library book', but could not stay to study: 'The University does not allow students to undertake prolonged study with their children within any part of the Library' (University of Bradford, 2018).

To take forward the library team's vision of creating a family study room in the library, a small task and finish project group was set up. The project group was led by the library's associate director and the library customer services manager. Library staff were asked to volunteer if they were interested in working on the project. The two volunteers from the customer services team and subject librarian team both have young children.

Student consultation and sector research

The project group started by further scoping out the project through discussing the idea with the student union sabbatical team. They expressed great enthusiasm for the idea, as they were very aware of the increasing number of students juggling studies and childcare, and of student parents/carers bringing small children onto the campus, often due to an unexpected breakdown in childcare arrangements. The project group did not have a way of identifying which students or staff are parents/carers of small children as this information is not held in student or staff records, so the student union sabbatical officers agreed to support the library team in gauging potential interest in a family study room by disseminating a link to a survey through one of their student updates.

The survey received only five replies. However, the detailed responses reinforced the project group's determination to go ahead with developing a family-friendly study space in the library. In particular, one respondent wrote about a child with ADHD and autism disturbing other students, the project group felt that creating a dedicated, protected space rather than having an open area would go some way towards creating a space where a parent/carer could study alongside their child without fear of their noise or behaviour disturbing other library users.

Bearing in mind that the starting point with the current university policy was not to allow children in the library at all (other than to pick up/drop off a book), one person responded that they generally spent more than two hours in the library with their child. The question on what they liked about visiting the library with their children produced a couple of positive replies: 'I love to see them engaged with reading', and, 'Convenient, have all resources around me that I need, no worries about childcare. Spend more time with the children and they can see what I do and take an interest. They can get their homework done while I study'. Others replied, 'I have never brought my children in the library, I wish I could', and, 'I don't, my child has additional needs in the form of ADHD and autism and wouldn't sit still'. Responses to the question what they did not like about visiting the library with their children included: 'Not much choice, difficult to keep them quiet for extended periods of time', and 'The fact that my child has ADHD and a library expects quiet for an impulse child is just not an option, I wouldn't get anything done because of behaviour management'. The library's no food policy was also cited:

> [N]o food policy it is ridiculous especially having to explain to your child they can't eat in here, 'Why mummy?' I don't know son it's just a rule, so the cleaners don't have to clean so much I suppose. Children require snacks, etc. to keep occupied, especially when they need it, having to constantly leave the library so they can eat is a major inconvenience.

A bookable dedicated space was preferred to a non-bookable space by four out of the five students, and one student commented, 'I don't feel the university accommodates for parents especially with additional needs. It affects your engagement, yet you don't support this. I attempted to get help in form of a support plan and was told I couldn't.'

The student survey was complemented by the library group carrying out further research into academic libraries' approaches to supporting student parents/carers with young children. A review of the literature found very little information on support for families in UK (United Kingdom) academic libraries but did reinforce the findings from the University of East London (Clover, 2017) that academic libraries in the US are leading the way in this area. A detailed review article (Keyes, 2017) was particularly useful in providing numerous positive examples of child-friendly spaces in US academic libraries and there was useful discussion about how to address health and safety and liability issues (both concerns at Bradford); the benefits of supporting parenting students were also clearly expressed:

> Academic libraries serve many student constituents, but one often overlooked group is students who are parenting children. Students who, by necessity or volition, bring their children with them to the library have specific needs. Serving these students, who often have difficulty succeeding and graduating at college, should be a priority for academic libraries. Offering assistance can help this group focus on their studies, achieve their academic goals, and thus decrease universities' attrition rates. The academic library is uniquely situated to make small changes to its space and/or policies to support parenting students' ability to balance school and family, and ultimately successfully complete their studies.
>
> (Keyes, 2017: 319)

Some US libraries have even introduced built-in cots into study desks. Bradford's project group felt this might be a step too far at present!

A call out for information via the JISC (Joint Information Systems Committee) library mailing list LIS-Link gained a lot of replies; however, most respondents were not currently offering any dedicated family space but wanting to know more about the idea. Some libraries stated an explicit 'Children in the Library' policy, while not offering a dedicated family study space to allow parents/carers to study in the library with their children. The University of Hull and University of Sussex both provided inspiring information about their well-established library family study rooms and shared invaluable information on their approach to regulating the space and health and safety considerations. They provided reassurance that their rooms were well used, and they had not encountered any problems or health and safety issues. Hull's family room was opened in October 2021, recognising that: 'A third of our student population are mature learners, many of whom are also managing family life as well as academic studies.' Hull staff also recommended ensuring that the room provided is dedicated for family use only: 'What we did have at first is students booking and attending without children – they just thought it was a nice room to use! Despite it clearly saying when booking that it is for family use.' Sussex University's library family room has been in place for several years and is a larger space for a maximum of 10 adults and 10 children or 15 adults. They also confirmed: 'We have had the family room for some years now and I don't think we have any concerns.' They helpfully provided their risk assessment for their room. While in the process of setting up University of Bradford's family study room, Bradford's project group also became aware of the library at the University of York setting up a family study room which, again, is a much bigger, shared study space with half of the room given over for students with children to work and the other half for children to play.

Advocacy to change the University Children on Campus Policy

In initial scoping discussions with the University of Bradford's directorate of infrastructure health and safety (H&S) team about changing the Children on Campus guidance, the H&S team voiced serious concerns about setting up a dedicated library family study room, with concern expressed that this would lead to students leaving children unsupervised in the room. To counter these concerns and influence the required change to the University Children on Campus Policy, the project group had to undertake advocacy work, including submitting a paper setting out the aims of the family study space to the University's executive board. This was accompanied by an equality impact assessment which, alongside the paper, clearly showed the positive impact that developing a family-supportive space within the library would have and demonstrated clear alignment with the University's stated EDI strategic goal to promote an inclusive working and learning environment at the University. The positive impact of the initiative on students without children was also stressed, as this would help to prevent them potentially being disturbed by noise from small children in an adult study space. The reviewers of the equality impact assessment did make some suggestions to further expand the library's plans, for example providing bottle-warming facilities and fridges for safe storage of milk for breastfeeding mothers; however, the project group decided to keep the initial concept simpler and therefore more manageable to set up.

Once the principle of a change to the University Children on Campus Policy had been accepted by the executive board, the project group started to work with the directorate of infrastructure on the practical considerations and challenges around creating a safe environment, risk assessment and procurement considerations in setting up the new space suitable for babies and young children.

Practical considerations in setting up a family-friendly study space

The project group identified a small group study room on the ground floor of the library which could be repurposed as a family study room. The room was previously used by small groups, up to six students. It is near the main library counter and opposite a toilet with baby-changing facilities. Due to potential safeguarding issues and the small size of the room available, it was agreed that a safe, enclosed bookable space was needed, where staff and student parents/carers could ensure their children were not disturbing other students, for example by running around or being noisy. The room, due to its small size, is bookable by one family group at a time. Its capacity is four people, one of whom must be an adult parent/carer, but could be two adults and up to two children under 12 years old, or one adult and one child over 12 years old. Any other family arrangement must be agreed in advance with library staff.

The room offers:

- child-sized furniture and books/colouring sheets for children;
- desk space for parent/carer and older children to study;
- space for a buggy/pram;
- 'Breastfeeding welcome here' signage, and a suitable chair provided for breastfeeding mothers.

Eating in the library, including in the family study room, is now permitted (not hot food), and large waste bins are provided just outside the room.

Directorate of infrastructure staff advised on developing robust room-booking protocols and signage providing clear rules for use of the room. This involved developing an immensely detailed risk assessment to create a study space suitable for babies and young children and proved very different to setting up a study area for adult library users, as it required a range of additional child safety features, including:

- corner protectors for the bookcase;
- tables with rounded corners;
- low-level bookcase secured to the wall so it cannot be pulled forward;
- 'child-sized' activity table and chairs provided for children's use, sourced from a specialist supplier of furniture for children's settings;
- covers for power sockets;
- finger guard for the door and slow-closing door to allow time for buggies and small children to pass through.

Cleaning products used by the cleaning team are the same as those used in the University nursery and so are suitable for settings where children are present.

The customer services team's opening routines at the start of each day include checking the room to ensure that it remains in a safe condition.

Initially the project group planned to include toys such as Lego® or soft toys in the room, but this was not agreed to, due to possible choking hazards and the difficulty of keeping soft toys clean. The project group also wanted to offer longer opening hours than those initially agreed to by the directorate for infrastructure. At present, the room is available for use only when the library team is working, 9 am to 5 pm on weekdays. The library team will keep this under review to see if the hours can safely be extended to weekends and early evening, when it may well be in demand. The colours used in the room are gender neutral and the children's books and even the rug with pictures of children from around the world emphasise the inclusive nature of the new space. Book titles include:

- *This Beach Is Loud*, by Samantha Cotterill, a book written to support children who are on the autistic spectrum or suffering from sensory processing disorders;
- *One Day So Many Ways*, by Laura Hall and Loris Lara, which covers a day in the life of 40 children around the world;
- *Golden Domes and Silver Lanterns: A Muslim Book of Colours*, by Hena Khan and Mehrdokht Amini, a picture book aiming to inspire conversations about world religions and cultures.

Figure 7.1 *The family study room* (photo: A. Lahlafi).

Right from the start, one of the main concerns of the directorate of infrastructure was that a parent/carer would leave a child unsupervised, or a child might go missing on campus. Several control measures were agreed to mitigate this risk.

- Access to the room is via an electronic lock which is controlled by card access mediated by library staff. During bookable hours the lock is active to students who have formally registered to use the room; it is active to staff from the library, security, cleaning and other maintenance teams at all times.
- The room can be used only by students who have registered to use it. The online registration form requires users to agree to a number of conditions before processing. One of these is to agree to supervise their child at all times and not leave them unattended (University of Bradford, n.d.). If any of the room-use conditions are not followed, the user may be stopped from making further bookings.
- As part of the booking process the library team takes a mobile telephone number for the booker, so if a child is left alone in the room the team can contact the parent/carer and get them to return and collect their child.
- Once their booking is processed the student receives a confirmatory e-mail, which reiterates the booking conditions, and the requirement for constant supervision of children.
- A notice on the door advises people to book so as to ensure that they can stay for the desired length of time.
- A notice inside the room explains the room's use and reiterates the booking conditions, including the requirement for adult supervision of children throughout.
- A notice inside the room advises on the nearest baby-changing facility and first aid station.
- A fetch service is offered. Parents/carers can request books in advance to collect on arrival, so there is no temptation to nip out of the room to fetch a book, leaving a child unattended.
- A written procedure has been developed to deal with a report of a missing child so that prompt action can be taken to locate them. This plan is initiated immediately upon a report of a missing child.

The high level of detail required in planning the room is exemplified by another area of risk identified: risk of injury/illness from items in the room such as injury from unsuitable toys or toxic crayons. Further control measures were introduced:

- Toys are not provided; any left in the room will be removed during daily checks.
- Only a selection of children's books, crayons and colouring sheets are provided. Only non-toxic (and washable) crayons are provided for use in the room. Broken crayons are removed on the daily room check.
- The terms and conditions of room use require users to leave the room in a clean and tidy state, and to report any problems to library staff at the start of their booking. Notices to this effect are displayed in the room and direct users to suitable waste bins close to the room.

The room was finally opened in late summer 2023. The opening event was designed by the library group to help raise awareness of the new space among key staff in the University. Everyone attending was given a printed promotional flier designed by a colleague in the customer services team. The room was officially opened by the pro-vice chancellor for EDI, and the pro-vice chancellor for learning, teaching and student experience. Other staff

invited included marketing staff – who later interviewed a student who regularly uses the room (Saleema, 2023), EDI colleagues, the University nursery managers, directorate of infrastructure staff and the education sabbatical officer for the Students' Union. The nursery managers promoted the library family study room to all parents of children that attend the University nursery, and recently collaborated with the library team to host World Book Day reading events for nursery children in the family study room as part of our outreach activities.

At the time of writing, the room has been open just over six months. It has been used by both University staff and students. Initial feedback has been extremely positive with five-star feedback reviews and repeat bookings showing that the room is proving a great success in supporting staff and students with their children. One respondent asked for an operator chair to be

Figure 7.2 *University of Bradford Students' Union education sabbatical officer holds a promotional flier at the official opening of the library family study room* (photo: K. Carver)

provided at the table in addition to the other chairs; this was immediately put into place. Feedback is gathered in several ways:

- verbally, to library staff;
- via Post-It notes on a whiteboard in the room;
- via an online form – a QR code link to the form is posted in the room and included via an e-mail which is sent out to users of the room one hour after their room booking ends.

The following are examples of feedback received from parents/carers:

It is such a beautiful idea to create a space for families in the library. It is very child friendly, neat and cosy.

It happened to be a good place for my baby, for fun with lots of attractive books today. Thanks for this privilege. All I can say now is 'good job and keep the good work on'.

This is truly a game changer for parents in University. A big thanks to the brains behind this.

It's really, really helpful. It engages the kids. It takes a lot of stress away from me. I used to think 'how do I cope with my studies and my child?' I was worried before I used to come to this room. It has released my stress dramatically. I hope that more students get to know about this space. I'm excited by this room. It's really brilliant. I love how cheerful the room is. I'm so happy.

A new policy for children on the University campus

The library team's raising of issues about the University Children on Campus Policy at the start of 2022, significantly, led to wider discussion across the University and helped to highlight that it was time to review the policy and ensure that it aligned with the University's emphasis on inclusion. A new policy was subsequently published in November 2023. The new policy has a clearly stated aim to 'ensure that staff, students and visitors are clear on their roles and responsibilities when navigating a range of scenarios that may arise and that any activities involving children on campus are conducted responsibly and within a clear, safe and supportive framework'. In reaching a view on whether an environment on campus is appropriate for the child, the policy now encourages a more inclusive approach, with consideration of individual circumstances and settings. The following criteria are stated, which align with the approach taken by the project group working in partnership with directorate of infrastructure colleagues to repurpose library study space:

- **Safe:** Is the area restricted or hazardous in any way? Can this be mitigated? Could the safety of colleagues or students be put at risk by the presence of the child(ren)?
- **Space:** Is there enough physical space for the child(ren) to be present without compromising their safety and comfort, or the safety and comfort of others?
- **Suitability:** Is the activity age appropriate for the child(ren), even if they will not be participating directly? For example, taking a toddler to a silent study area would likely disrupt other users of that space. Equally, an older child may be able to sit quietly in a lecture theatre, but the content of the session may not be appropriate for a non-adult audience, creating an emotional challenge for them.
- **Student and staff impact:** Has the comfort and potential impact on fellow staff and/or students been considered? Where possible, have other students or staff been consulted about accommodating a child in the space/activity?
- **Support:** If applicable, is there any support that could be provided/signposted which could assist the responsible adult in sourcing childcare, either now or in the future?

Conclusion

Working closely with directorate of infrastructure, estates, H&S and EDI colleagues across the University on planning and realising a new family study room has emphasised the key role the library plays in providing safe, inclusive study space to support all our students and staff. The library team continue to keep a watching brief on UK higher education libraries' support for parents/carers, as a small number of them are now opening family study rooms. In October 2023 the Scottish Confederation of University and Research Libraries EDI Network launched a toolkit to support member libraries in embedding good practice consistently across services (SCURL, 2023). This provided three examples of family study lounges (University of Strathclyde, University of Glasgow and Edinburgh Napier University) which provide similar provision to Bradford's family study room. It is clear that some other university library family spaces do offer larger spaces, spaces that are not always bookable, a range of toys and longer opening hours. Although most can be used only if children are with the parent/carer, some do open the study space more widely to all students if it is not in use by parent/carers with their children. At Bradford there will be continued monitoring of usage and analysis of feedback to see what further improvements can be brought to the space and whether the current opening hours and one-family-at-a-time approach are sufficient to meet University of Bradford staff and student demand. At the time of writing the University is also awaiting the outcome of a bid submitted to Academic Libraries North (ALN) for EDI innovation funding to support a collaborative project with another university library to evaluate our family study rooms. The project would focus on evaluation of current family study provision and produce a family room toolkit to be hosted online on the ALN website to guide and advise other ALN libraries that would like to establish their own provision.

References

BBC (2023) University of Bradford Tops List for Social Mobility for Third Year, www.bbc.co.uk/news/education-67145398.

Clover, D. (2017) Meeting the Needs of Parents and Carers within Library Services: Responding to Student Voices at the University of East London, *SCONUL Focus*, **68**, 26–9, https://access.sconul.ac.uk/publication/meeting-the-needs-of-parents-and-carers-within-library-services.

HEPI (2023) 2023 English Social Mobility Index, www.hepi.ac.uk/2023/10/19/2023-english-social-mobility-index.

Keyes, K. (2017) Welcoming Spaces: Supporting Parenting Students at the Academic Library, *The Journal of Academic Librarianship*, **43** (4), 319–28.

Saleema, H. (2023) University of Bradford Launches New Family Study Room, *Telegraph & Argus*, 24 November, www.thetelegraphandargus.co.uk/news/23944959.university-bradford-launches-new-family-study-room.

SCURL (2023) Library Environment Inclusive Study Space, www.scurl.ac.uk/edi-toolkit-student-experience#Library-Environment.

University of Bradford (2018) University Children on Campus Policy.

University of Bradford (2020) Making Our Diversity Count: Equality, Diversity and Inclusion Strategy 2020–25.

University of Bradford (n.d.) Library Spaces, bradford.ac.uk/library/contact-and-about-us/library-spaces.

University of Bradford: Centre for Inclusion and Diversity (2023) Policy: Children on Campus.

8

Politics, Persuasion and Persistence: The Learning Commons Project at the University of Galway

John Cox

Introduction

The unifying theme of this case study is the experience of advocating for and planning the Learning Commons building at the University of Galway across a period of 25 years. During that time a series of major changes has shaped the specification and, indeed, the concept of the building. These changes have originated in a mix of local and global factors. Locally, institutional estates strategy, the direction of growth of the campus, rises in student numbers, a far more diverse and demanding student population and evolving priorities in the strategy of the University have been major influencers. Changes from without, notably global emphasis on equality, diversity and inclusion as well as sustainability, and, in higher education especially, new approaches to teaching and learning, have had a significant impact. These have sat alongside new building regulations, construction industry inflation and technological evolution. User needs and expectations are fundamental to the design of any library building, and these too have changed hugely, mandating the inclusion of a very different range and distribution of spaces from those envisaged in the late 1990s.

Advocacy for reimagining the library building at the University of Galway has needed to evolve and to accommodate different political circumstances across two and a half decades. If the range of factors outlined above has shaped the building, politics have driven the direction of the project at large through a series of ups and downs, changes in institutional leadership, harnessing of student support, engagement with local politicians and the timing of funding opportunities. Stakeholder management, upwards, downwards and across, has been vital, as has been the need to adapt both the approach to advocacy and its content according to different situations. Some key moments have needed to be navigated and sometimes confronted robustly.

This case study therefore emphasises the journey rather than the destination, which has not yet been reached. It narrates a story of change, first to the specification and nature of the building itself and then in the approach to advancing the project across multiple constituencies and shifting political climates.

The University of Galway

Founded in 1845, the University of Galway is located on the west coast of Ireland and has over 19,000 students and 2,500 staff. It is a research-intensive university, and its four colleges cover a wide range of academic specialisms to offer a broad choice of teaching programmes at undergraduate and postgraduate level. The University has a unique role in promoting and sustaining teaching and research in the Irish language. Its strategy to 2025 is founded on core values of respect, excellence, openness and sustainability. International engagement is a priority, as is sustainable development; the University is in the top 50 institutions in the *Times Higher Education* Impact Rankings.

The Main Library building, the James Hardiman Library, was built in 1973 at the heart of the campus and occupies almost 10,000 m², with 1,860 study spaces. Since 2013 it has been adjoined by the Hardiman Research Building, which is shared with research institutes in the arts, humanities and social sciences and includes over 3,000 m² of library space, primarily for archives and special collections. There are also two separate libraries: the Medical Library in the Clinical Sciences Institute at University Hospital Galway and the library of Shannon College of Hotel Management beside Shannon Airport. A new Learning Commons building will be located a few minutes' walk from the James Hardiman Library and will replace it when completed.

Chronology of key library building developments

Table 8.1 opposite summarises the major milestones on the 25-year journey so far to the Learning Commons at the University of Galway.

Developments in the construction environment

Campus estates strategy

Numerous changes have impacted on the construction environment since 1999, some local and others global. Locally, the University's estates strategy has seen a major building programme to accommodate higher student numbers and new areas of research and teaching. The emphasis for some time was on constructing new buildings, but recent institutional strategies have promoted the regeneration of existing space. New buildings needed new space and a revised master plan resulted in the development of a North Campus, as shown on the University campus map (University of Galway, 2023). This changed the geography of the campus such that the Main Library

Table 8.1 *Summary of key library building developments at University of Galway*

Year	Development	Significance
1999	Main library extended	20% (1,800 m²) space addition
2000	'Blueprint for the Future of the Library' study completed	Space deficits highlighted and future options outlined
2006	'Resourcing Research and Enabling Learning in the 21st Century' study completed	Feasibility study recommended but not activated
2008	New Arts, Humanities and Social Sciences Research building, incorporating archives, announced	New provision promised for research support in designated disciplines
2009	Nursing Library extension added to Main Library	600 m² added
2013	Opening of Arts, Humanities and Social Sciences Research building	Major upgrade and academic embedding of heritage collections facilities
2014	Library building feasibility report, 'Transformation of Existing Facilities', completed	Costed building transformation plan agreed as feasible and needed, but unfunded
2018	Students' Union campaign, including national media coverage, about library building inadequacy	Highlighting of student discontent on and beyond the campus regarding library space deficits
2019	Library building transformation project selected for submission to government call for facilities funding	First-time institutional prioritisation of library building upgrade
2019	University funding bid successful	Main library building transformation project funded
2020	Main library capacity reduced to 150 study spaces via COVID-19 restrictions	Previously over-compressed use of building exposed
2021	Planning for transformed library building, including Bookbot, at advanced stage	Budget increased to accommodate Bookbot, freeing up space via automated storage and retrieval of collections
2022	Decision to build new Learning Commons instead of library transformation agreed	Greater flexibility and fundraising potential with less user disruption
2022	Student numbers reach 20,000, almost double 1999 figure	Major pressure on space
2023	Building size retained at 10,100 m² instead of newly proposed 8,000 m²	Future proofing
2023	Planning permission secured	Potential delays obviated, as no objection to planning emerged

is today located in the middle of the South Campus rather than at the centre of the whole estate. The thrust of national funding for much of this period favoured research, and the new buildings at the University of Galway reflected this. One of these was the Hardiman Research Building for the humanities and social sciences, which opened in 2013, adjoining the Main Library and transforming its facilities for archives and special collections and related research services.

The emphasis on new buildings in the campus estates strategy left little scope for progress in improving the existing Main Library beyond the addition of a Nursing and Midwifery Library in 2009. However, the deterioration of the Main Library and its inability to meet the evolving needs of a larger student population were recognised through the commissioning of a feasibility study completed in 2014. This study asserted the need for a major physical intervention to transform the building, alongside costings and a project plan. University leadership acknowledged the business case for transforming the Main Library, but the required funding did not become available. There was instead an increased emphasis towards distributing study spaces, notably in new student residences, or developing more versatile spaces to support group study and more social, collaborative learning methods within academic buildings across the campus. These developments were concerning because they appeared to put a brake on transforming the Main Library building, previously identified as the primary space for learning across all disciplines.

Standards and regulations

Globally, the sustainable development of the planet has come to the forefront in recent years. Sustainability is one of the University's core values in its current strategy, reflecting a long-standing institutional commitment which includes a target to achieve carbon neutrality by 2050. Building standards in Ireland have evolved to mandate sustainable development, and the adoption of the Nearly Zero Energy Building (NZEB) standard (Sustainable Energy Authority of Ireland, 2019) requires a very high energy performance, with maximum use of energy from renewable sources. This requirement is more easily delivered by new buildings and was a factor in the decision in 2022 to construct a new Learning Commons instead of transforming the existing Main Library building. Sustainability, including BREEAM (Building Research Establishment Environmental Assessment Methodology) accreditation at the Excellent level, is a key focus for the Learning Commons. It will aim to meet demanding energy efficiency targets and will include a range of features such as green roof space, prioritised pedestrian and cyclist infrastructure, biodiversity amenity space and sustainable drainage.

The regulatory environment for construction in Ireland has changed considerably since 2000. Irish building regulations are closely aligned with those applying in the United Kingdom (UK). The publication of a series of regulations has progressively tightened oversight and quality control for construction projects and increased requirements and specifications for buildings, with a particular emphasis on fire safety and accessibility for people with disabilities. Fire safety regulations have impacted on a range of specifications, including structural fire resistance, stair width, evacuation lifts and materials used in construction. Accessibility regulations are related, and include the requirement since 2010 for a Disability Access Certificate (DAC) in all instances where new works are commencing or where a Fire Safety Certificate is required. The DAC demonstrates that adequate provision has been made for people with disabilities to access and circulate around the premises. A point of particular significance for the Learning Commons project has been the mandating of much more generous provision of space between rows of study desks and of bookshelves in new or regenerated buildings than had been the practice in the Main Library. The impact of this on the number of study spaces able to be accommodated was influential in discussions around constructing a new Learning Commons building.

Pandemic effects

The COVID-19 pandemic turned the focus even more sharply on the capacity of the Main Library. Restrictions introduced on reopening in summer 2020 resulted in a dramatic reduction in the number of study spaces from 1,860 to 150. Social distancing and other protective measures exposed the way in which study spaces had been compressed into the building through small desk sizes with minimal space between them so as to wring maximum capacity from a facility struggling to keep up with rising student numbers. The reduction in capacity was far greater than at any other university library in Ireland and generated huge dissatisfaction among the student body, reflected in a significant drop in the LibQUAL (Association of Research Libraries, 2024) survey scores for the 'Library as Place' dimension in spring 2021. Consequently, an increase in the number of study spaces of all types became a big part of the conversation around the Main Library building project. The COVID-19 experience was certainly influential in the change of direction towards constructing a new Learning Commons.

Academic libraries also enjoyed some gains from the pandemic, notably in reinforcing their vital social function as a place of community on campus, with positive impact on the well-being of their users at a time of isolation for many people (Cox and Benson-Marshall, 2021). Despite student disgruntlement with the low capacity of the Main Library, it became clear that there was limited appetite for using study spaces provided at alternative locations on campus. This helpfully reinforced the status of the library as the preferred learning space for students at the University of Galway, adding further impetus to, and goodwill towards, the building project. Experience with COVID-19 has shaped planning for the new Learning Commons in several ways, notably generosity of furniture size and spacing in the event of a future pandemic, provision of facilities for hybrid meetings and the inclusion of hotdesking arrangements for staff. The latter will represent a new departure relative to previous plans, but also a more efficient use of valuable space, which is likely to be a key part of estates strategy at this and many other campuses (Cox, 2023).

COVID-19 also contributed to a sharp rise in inflation from 2020, another major influence on the construction environment worldwide with significant implications for the Learning Commons project. The Society of Chartered Surveyors Ireland (SCSI) (2024) has tracked construction industry inflation in Ireland over a lengthy period through its Tender Price Index, conveniently taking 1998 as its base year with a value of 100 and thereby coinciding closely with the 25-year period used in this chapter. Earlier activation of construction on the Main Library project would have cost the University substantially less, especially in the period 2011–16, when the commercial building index ranged between 100 and 125. On either side of that window there were rises to 150 in 2006, before the global economic recession struck, and from 150 in 2018 to 210 at the end of 2023, with costs driven rapidly upwards by COVID-19, Brexit, war in Ukraine and other factors. Inflation has been an issue of ongoing concern throughout this project at the University of Galway, with an increase to its budget voted in 2021 to align with rising costs. Concerns are never far away that value engineering may compromise the finished product as project funding chases cost increases.

Technology

It is also worth mentioning the opportunities afforded by developments in building and library technology since the late 1990s. Building management technologies have advanced significantly in that period and artificial intelligence promises further possibilities for monitoring environmental conditions and space usage, as well as enabling efficient, data-driven energy management. Technology will be key to the success of the Learning Commons building. Users will expect ubiquitous and fast network access, spaces for digital creativity and access to technologies too expensive to be offered for public use elsewhere on campus for purposes such as data manipulation and making objects. The versatility of the building to accommodate the range of spaces required by a large user community with diverse needs will be enabled by a transformative collection management technology in the shape of the Bookbot. This technology frees up a lot of extra space by enabling automated storage and retrieval of printed collections, which can be located remotely rather than on library floors. It is discussed later, in the section on changes to the building concept and specification.

User needs and expectations

The needs and expectations of users today are different in many ways as compared with those of 25 years ago, although it is important to be aware of some fundamentally unchanged requirements too. A much increased and more diverse student body, new approaches to teaching and learning and heightened emphasis on equality, diversity and inclusion have combined to shape the design of the Learning Commons building as a far more versatile and dynamic learning environment than had been envisaged in the late 1990s.

Changing student population

The University of Galway has experienced a surge in student numbers since the turn of the century. In 1999/2000 the number of registered students was 11,234, but by 2021/22 this had exceeded 20,000 for the first time, reaching 20,214. This almost doubling of the student body was accompanied by major changes in its composition, making it far more diverse. International students comprise 15.5% of the current student population, while the number of students registered with the University's disability support service has increased six-fold, from around 250 in 2006 to almost 1,500 more recently. Widening participation initiatives at government level mean that the student body is representative of a much wider range of socioeconomic backgrounds than previously.

A significantly larger student population has had implications for the Main Library building, the most obvious one being much greater pressure on available space, which has contributed to the tight compression of study spaces mentioned earlier. In addition, there is demand for a wider range of support to meet the needs of a more diverse group of users, with an expectation that libraries will host such services (Blummer and Kenton, 2017). The Main Library, with its long opening hours and convenient campus location, has been viewed as the optimal location for the Assistive Technology Service and the Academic Writing Centre, despite its limited and often inflexible space.

Equality, diversity and inclusion

Moving hand in hand with the diversification of the student body has been a strong societal momentum towards equality, diversity and inclusion. Higher education institutions have become much more cognisant of failings in their history in this regard and the need to ensure that their current policies and practice meet the highest standards. This cognisance extends to the library building and the messaging it conveys. Its architecture and imagery are under scrutiny in terms of potentially representing a dominant White and Global North perspective, while the inclusiveness or otherwise of the different spaces it houses is under examination. Andrew Cox (2023) captures these issues well, noting that certain designs can alienate library users from different cultures or can create feelings of exclusion among users with disabilities. He rightly notes the importance of extending the recognition of disability beyond the visible and physical to less visible cognitive and other differences, generating a range of sensory responses to library space.

Accessibility is a key factor in the planning of the Learning Commons at the University of Galway, extending to the provision of sensory areas, assistive technology and inclusive spaces such as gender-neutral toilet facilities, underpinned by universal design. There is also a much deeper understanding now than 25 years ago of the challenges, but also the importance, of creating a place of community and exposure to diverse experiences in which students from many different backgrounds can enjoy this building as part of an inclusive sense of their journey at the university. This should mean that they encounter no obstacles to access and feel included through the representation of diversity in the campus population, its events, art and architecture. Widening participation initiatives create a requirement to accommodate individual needs as far as possible, rather than viewing the library user community simply as a group or a conglomeration of groups (Odonnell and Anderson, 2022).

Teaching and learning

If increased student numbers, greater diversity in the student body and the emphasis on inclusivity have shaped the design of library buildings, developments in teaching and learning have fundamentally changed their concept. This has influenced the University towards the idea of a new Learning Commons building. Approaches to teaching and learning have changed radically worldwide in recent decades, including at the University of Galway via the leadership of the Centre for Excellence in Learning and Teaching (CELT). There has been a shift in emphasis from didactic to constructivist teaching, from passive to experiential learning and from information consumption towards knowledge creation, often through teamwork rather than individual effort alone. The focus is on participation, interaction and independent activity through problem-based learning, group assignments and collaborative, peer-to-peer working, all enabled by a diverse and evolving series of technologies.

A reconceptualisation of library buildings to support this new range of activities and expectations has occurred, and the Learning Commons will reflect this. It will be characterised by ubiquitous technology, a makerspace and other facilities to foster digital creativity, varied spaces for group work and the hosting of a range of campus services to support student learning success. The overarching aim will be to provide a diversity of spaces to meet preferred learning styles. Some elements of continuity will be important in this regard, including the provision of quiet spaces for individual work, still highly valued by students. Planning for study spaces in the Learning Commons is being guided by research by Gensler (2015) indicating that students focus on individual work over collaborative activity by a factor of three to one.

User concerns

User sentiment through surveys and other feedback across more than two decades has been clear in its frustration at the inadequacy of the Main Library relative to expectations. The building has been unable to keep pace with changing needs and has for some time failed even on the basics, much less the demand for newer spaces and facilities. The lack of a sufficient number of study spaces has been highlighted consistently in surveys since 1999, and comparisons with other Irish university libraries have shown a very noticeable lag in terms of seats per student. Other deficits featuring regularly in user feedback throughout the period have included access for users with disabilities, air quality, temperature control and availability of power and data points. Some concerns have been replaced by others over time, with spacing of books on shelves featuring in 1999, but not afterwards, and the level of provision of access to social spaces emerging as a deficiency in 2018. One unchanging pattern has been visible in local responses to the LibQUAL survey since 2010, with ratings of the 'Library as Place' dimension trailing those for the rest of the survey and dragging down overall satisfaction scores. This has been the case despite a strong student preference for the library building as a place of study, with over one million user visits annually and a combined daily or weekly visit figure of 78.1% for undergraduates in 2023, higher than the 77.6% recorded in 2006.

The year 2018 proved significant in highlighting user disgruntlement. A survey of academic staff, conducted by CELT in November of that year, found that 92% of respondents believed that the library building needed investment to fulfil its role in supporting learning, with individual comments referencing many limitations. The Students' Union featured the poor quality of the building on the front page of its newsletter in the same month. Although the university won government funding in 2019 to transform the existing Main Library, a subsequent event in the shape of the COVID-19 pandemic and the huge reduction of study spaces available under social distancing restrictions proved highly significant. The relevant LibQUAL scores dropped sharply, and this contributed to a rethink about the best approach for the future, recognising that a new building could deliver over 350 extra study spaces relative to the existing project, which would barely retain the current number even with all possible optimisations. This was a major change in scope for the building project and is featured in the next section.

An evolving building concept and specification

Three developments have combined to shape the Main Library building project in ways not considered at its outset 25 years ago. These are identification of the space as a learning commons, the introduction of a Bookbot for collection storage and retrieval and the decision to construct a new building instead of regenerating the existing one.

From library to learning commons

The learning commons concept came into vogue from the mid-2000s onwards (Blummer and Kenton, 2017). It succeeded the information commons, which emphasised access to computer facilities within a library or library-like facility, by offering a more versatile and broadly based value proposition. In a learning commons, spaces, technology and staff are organised primarily around the delivery of wider learning objectives. Technology is an enabler of learning rather than an end in itself and learners are supported through partnerships between a range of parties. These include library staff, academics, learning technologists and specialists in areas such as academic writing and mathematics. The learning commons facility aligns well with the move towards more collaborative, participative, problem-based and creative learning described earlier.

Two drivers promoted its adoption at the University of Galway. Firstly, the emphasis on new research buildings on campus had begun to shift in favour of student-focused facilities. Specifically, the opening in 2013 of the Hardiman Research Building adjoining the Main Library moved the focus of the latter facility and the project to redevelop it towards serving undergraduate needs primarily. Secondly, when the opportunity to pitch for government funding emerged in 2019, differentiation was important. The bid was framed around the idea of a learning commons as a point of distinction to attract funder attention, since no other entire university library building in Ireland was thus designated.

The funding bid was successful, but transforming the existing Main Library building into a true learning commons facility proved problematic and necessitated the two other major changes in building specification described in the rest of this section. The learning commons identity has remained constant, however, and raises a few questions to which clear answers have yet to emerge. Will users, especially academic staff, readily adopt this new terminology and concept when the building opens? How best will fundraising navigate potentially divergent inclinations among prospective donors, in some cases towards the traditional and still powerful library brand, in others towards the distinctive and 'buzzy' learning commons? Ultimately, will the building simply be called the Learning Commons or will it also incorporate the word 'library' in its name?

Collections storage and retrieval technology

Bookbot, or automated storage and retrieval system (ASRS), technology allows books to be stored at high density in a closed access area and retrieved on demand, typically within 15 minutes of the request. McCaffrey (2021) comprehensively describes its implementation at the University of Limerick. One vendor has estimated that seven times more books can be stored than via traditional library shelving (Dematic, 2016), a figure which attracted strong interest at Galway. Very limited expansion space, alongside the need to distribute seating and shelving further apart to meet revised accessibility requirements in current Irish building regulations, had emerged as major issues. The project was facing an outcome which would realise fewer study spaces than before and would fall short of the far more varied range of facilities for learning outlined in the university's successful bid for government funding in 2019. The Bookbot model became central to enabling the building to meet expectations by facilitating a huge reduction in the footprint occupied by collections. This will ensure rapid access on demand, while allowing the freed-up floor area to be filled by a diversity of user-facing spaces. A bid for extra funding to integrate this technology into the project was successful in mid-2021.

A point of difference in the proposed implementation is that the intention is for the Bookbot to house the majority of the library's collections, with a much-reduced number of volumes accessible on open shelving. It is more common for this type of system to provide supplementary storage rather than to become the main collections repository, something which will represent a major change for users when operational. This may generate a range of sentiments, but the heightened emphasis on the digital arising from the COVID-19 experience has supported a new perspective on balancing access to online and printed resources.

Redevelopment or new building?

An options analysis conducted in 2019 as part of the bid for government funding concluded that the transformation of the current Main Library building was the optimal approach, especially on grounds of sustainability. A new building at a site adjacent to the existing one had been considered in the late 1990s but estates strategy had now moved towards the regeneration of existing facilities. Some very significant problems emerged, however, as the design of the transformed Main Library progressed. These included:

* the limitations presented by a listed building in which the drive for transformation conflicted with moves to conserve existing spaces;
* a general inflexibility exacerbated by multiple extensions which had spawned a series of additional stairways and other suboptimal uses of space;
* insufficient user space, meaning that only the same number of study spaces could be realised even with the optimisations offered by the Bookbot;
* very limited potential for current or future expansion;
* likelihood of major disruption to users, with work planned on a floor-by-floor basis while the building remained open in the absence of alternative library space on campus;
* uncertainties regarding the timescale for construction, given the scale of the intervention, which included the introduction of an atrium.

A new director of the Buildings and Estates Department joined the University at what proved to be an opportune moment in October 2021, bringing a fresh perspective by proposing the construction of a new building on a site just a few minutes' walk towards the North Campus from the current library building and retaining its centrality. This was an appealing potential solution, addressing some major concerns already outlined at a similar projected cost. The new building, although only a little bigger than the existing one, offered significantly more capacity through better use of space, potentially enabling an additional 350 study spaces to be provided and integrating the Bookbot instead of housing it separately. Substantial room for future expansion was afforded by the new site. There would be no disruption to users, who could continue in the Main Library while the new Learning Commons was built to a much more predictable timetable. The new building would score much more highly in the critical areas of accessibility and sustainability, all at an attractive location affording views over the River Corrib, uniting the North and South campuses, strengthening linkage to the local community and offering a more compelling proposition to potential donors.

Despite its advantages, the proposed new direction generated some concerns too. Planning permission for a tall building close to some residential dwellings might be challenging to secure. Relocation of staff from other university departments occupying the site would be required. Busy traffic routes surrounded the new site, creating an imperative to ensure safe access. The proposal represented a major variation from that which had secured government investment and would need to be cleared with the funders. It was evident too that the archives and special collections should remain in their purpose-built facilities in the Hardiman Research Building, creating a separation from the new Learning Commons which was not ideal. Although the learnings from previous design work could be leveraged, some time would be lost in starting a whole new construction project, including a fresh round of procurement. Nevertheless, the opportunities offered by the new building were considered to outweigh the challenges by far, and, following a period of consultation, the University approved this major change in the project. The Learning Commons concept and building specification had evolved hugely over the project.

Advocacy, politics and pressure points
Sustaining the case for substantial investment in the Main Library building across two and a half decades has called for evolving the message, managing relations with key stakeholders and adapting leadership approaches to navigate key moments of opportunity and threat.

Making the case
Having a clear message has been vital throughout this period, but the content of the message and how to sell it have varied. A constant has been the alignment of the argument for investment with the needs of the institution at large and its strategy, rather than with those of the library specifically, always taking account of the wider higher education context. Avoiding an insular focus on library priorities and problems has been a first principle, placing the emphasis instead on opportunities for the University. The packaging of the message needs ongoing attention to keep it concise and effective, maximising imagery, infographics and bite-sized summaries of benefits rather than overloading advocacy documentation with dense text. Language also calls for careful thought to embed a compelling proposition,

for example through repeated references to the concepts of transformation, ambition, creativity, innovation and empowerment, all sited within the overarching idea of a distinctive student learning journey.

Pitching the case to different University presidents has required flexibility according to the priorities of the individuals concerned and their preferences for receiving information. In one case this involved a focus on data such as LibQUAL survey ratings, footfall patterns per discipline and comparative rankings of investment and experience at other institutions. The data were supplemented by arguments for enhancing institutional competitiveness within Ireland and internationally and for emulating in the Main Library the positive user experience resulting from recent investment in the Hardiman Research Building adjoining it. These issues were also of interest to the most recent president, but a less data-centric approach to advocacy had traction, alongside a narrative focused on the student experience, possibilities for teaching and learning, the library as a place of community on campus, regional connectivity and long-term legacy. The thrust of the present University strategy towards the public good, sustainability and well-being has also provided strong points of connection, with the values of librarianship such as diversity, equality of access and intellectual freedom, undoubtedly helping to advance the building project.

Managing and mobilising stakeholders

A major building initiative can only progress with the approval of the University president, and keeping the incumbent of the day interested and supportive has been an ongoing challenge. Managing relations with other stakeholders across and beyond the institution is also vital and has always been a major preoccupation. A priority for the University librarian was to maintain strong one-to-one relationships with individual members of the institutional leadership team, building goodwill, listening to and documenting their advice on how or when to act and seeking support at pressure points such as those described later in this chapter. The same has been true in relation to senior academics who wield influence with the president and leadership team, ensuring coverage across all disciplines and not just those with a strong tradition of library use.

Engaging and mobilising a large and growing student body around the library building as a priority among many competing issues has been challenging but critical to any chance of success, given its size and influence as the primary user group for this facility. The cultivation of good relations with the Students' Union, specifically its president and education officer, has proved effective. This was especially so in 2018/19 when the education officer, a mature student with invaluable political skills and connections, led a campaign to voice student agitation about the current building and the expectation of something far better. Winning support beyond the campus played an important part in the successful outcome of the University's funding bid in 2019. The University librarian, encouraged by the president, met with two local TDs (Teachtaí Dála, equivalent to Members of Parliament), both in senior government positions, initially to get advice on optimally pitching the funding bid. Ongoing contact with these two politicians saw them use their influence to keep it prominent in the thinking of decision makers, notably by facilitating the inclusion of a tour of the Main Library by the minister of state for higher education when she visited the campus in May 2019. Personal contact of this kind with the person having ultimate authority in the decision process proved vital.

A key development on campus, once the building project had commenced, was the formation of the Learning Commons Senior Stakeholder Group (LCSSG) in April 2021. This emanated from a recommendation following a quality review of the library two months earlier which identified a gap in the project governance. The review group perceived that the strong focus on the details of constructing the building risked missing out on a fuller engagement with stakeholder requirements. The overall objective of the LCSSG is to ensure that senior stakeholders in the University are informed of key developments relating to the Learning Commons project, can offer strategic guidance to the project and are able to support and champion it.

The LCSSG is chaired by the University president and comprises 21 members in senior positions across the University, with 11 of them being members of the University management team. It has representation from the main constituencies with a stake in the Learning Commons, including teaching and learning, research, the student body, equality, funding, estates and library. The LCSSG has had a huge impact on the project, steering it through some choppy waters and helping to ensure that the final version of the building will meet the strategic and operational needs of the University for the longer term. Very importantly, it has given the Learning Commons high visibility at senior leadership level and right across the campus, enabling stakeholders to influence the direction and quality of the building as the project progresses and before any major decisions are finalised. This, allied to multiple discussions and consultations with users and library staff about specific spaces, building on a campus-wide user survey in late 2020 and regular reports to the Library Strategy Committee, has created a sense of excitement around the project and of inclusion in its planning.

Library–estates interaction

The relationship between the library and the estates department is crucial to any library building project. As with most other aspects of the Learning Commons journey, this relationship has had its ups and downs during this project and each department has probably at times found the other a challenging stakeholder to manage. Both are members of the LCSSG, but the University librarian provides its secretariat and played the lead role in its establishment. The focus on construction identified by the library quality review group in early 2021 accurately reflects the situation at that time. The library team lacked experience with a project of this scale, so the buildings and estates representatives took the lead and quite understandably put its focus and that of the wider project team on the many complexities emerging from the effort to transform an inflexible building and the associated rise in costs at a time of high inflation. The LCSSG adjusted the balance significantly towards the influence of stakeholder perspectives in ways perhaps more warmly welcomed by the library as a department.

It may be that libraries and estates departments approach stakeholder engagement in a major construction project quite differently, and a sense of this has grown over time. Estates departments understand the end-to-end construction process intimately, including the challenges raised by competing or late-entry demands from a wide pool of stakeholders. Delivering the project on time and on budget is a primary area of focus and there have been times in this project when the University librarian had to take a contrary position in advocating for specification changes and extra funding to realise longer-term ambitions. This did not sit easily with those who estimated the original project cost, and may have wounded their professional pride. A situation of this nature may be an inevitable consequence of differing perspectives on stakeholder engagement, with libraries keen to harness continuously the widest possible range of views towards the ultimate design and estates departments aiming to reach a final specification for clarity.

Another tension in this project has been the extent to which the library team has been included in the wider aspects of the project beyond the design of spaces in the building. There has been a feeling of being kept at arm's length, with considerable periods of time elapsing without information, allied to a sense of being expected to jump to attention at short notice. Again, an amount of this is understandable, given the pressure on everyone, especially after the change of direction towards a new building and a concomitant desire to make up for lost time. This sat alongside the complex work involved in procurement and applying for planning permission, areas in which others are far better versed than staff in the library. Nevertheless, a more comprehensive approach to communication and a greater sense of inclusion of the library team as lead client can oil the wheels of good relations. The sense that others know best can be alienating and runs the risk of diminishing trust and goodwill. Teamwork is a better recipe for success than individual action or a sense of competition, as has been evident in successful collaborations to secure funding and to achieve university acceptance of the proposal for a new building.

Moments of truth for library leadership

The period since the late 1990s has seen several moments of particular significance to the future of the project, each requiring a different leadership approach from the University librarian. A strong case was made for investment in 2000/01 and 2005/06 following local working group reports, but action did not follow in either instance. A similar situation arose in 2014/15 following the report of an externally led feasibility study commissioned by the University. The need for investment was acknowledged both at the time and in the University strategy for 2015–20, but funding was not assigned. A key political factor was that the library as a department was seen already to have benefited, especially in terms of facilities for heritage collections, from the construction of the adjoining Hardiman Research Building earlier in that presidency. In each of these three cases the University librarian assembled and presented a strong argument but was unable to persuade the University to make a definite commitment in the face of competing priorities.

The next opportunity occurred in 2018/19 and elicited a change of approach from the University librarian. Three favourable developments came together within a short period. Firstly, a new president, taking up office early in 2018, had long embraced the centrality of libraries to campus life and identified the potential for investment in the Main Library building to transform the student learning experience. Secondly, the Students' Union, led by its education officer, began an active campaign in the autumn of 2018 to register its dissatisfaction with the condition of the library building and to demand action. This was a moment of truth in terms of leadership stance and the University librarian took a risk in joining forces with the Students' Union in that campaign. An early outcome was the publication of a front-page interview in the Union newspaper, subsequently published at national level in *The Irish Times* (Kenny, 2018), with a headline quoting that interview: 'Cramped, inflexible and uncomfortable. . . our students deserve better'.

Joining in with the student campaign, including some social media posts advocating investment, brought some censure from institutional leadership. However, given the lack of success at previous moments of opportunity, something different seemed necessary. National media coverage gained more traction than previous efforts at persuasion. When the third favourable development emerged, a government call for bids for capital projects in higher education in January 2019, the University for the first time prioritised the Main Library for its institutional submission and was successful in winning €15 million.

The situation emerging in mid-2021 constituted both a threat and an opportunity. As described earlier, the challenges of transforming an inflexible, listed building and complying with new building regulations had made clear a substantial shortfall in available space relative to the ambitions of the project. There was a reluctance from the buildings and estates department to seek additional funds relatively soon after the project had commenced, but from a library perspective this needed to be challenged. The issue at hand seemed to be a contest between keeping the project on budget or constructing the right building.

The recent formation of the LCSSG proved vital, as it provided a forum for debate and consultation by people at the top of the institution. The University librarian realised early the importance of acting independently in this situation, consulting individually with the president as LCSSG chair and with other members, as well as making a presentation to the University management team. The message remained simple, emphasising the importance of taking a long-term view and retaining ambition for a building vital to the whole University community. Having control of the presentation of options to the LCSSG enabled a demonstration of the consequences of adhering to the current plan and the opportunity presented by investing in a Bookbot to open up space. The support of the president, who had seen Bookbot technology in operation when planning a learning building in a previous role, proved crucial. The LCSSG strongly recommended that the project incorporate this technology, while recognising the extra cost entailed by it and more broadly via the sudden increase in construction price inflation. This outcome, and the subsequent voting of a large increase in the project budget by the University, was a positive signal and highlighted the value of taking an independent leadership approach and retaining ambition at a pressure point.

The University had embraced the opportunity to change the direction of the project towards a new building in early 2022, but the end of that year brought a serious threat to the viability of that facility. Members of the LCSSG learned that the size of the Learning Commons was now intended to be 8,000m² instead of 10,000m² as promised in the proposal for a new building. This reduction in capacity emerged in a presentation by the buildings and estates members and came as a surprise to all present, including the library representatives, with whom no prior consultation had taken place. Its consequences were stark, negating the impact of the Bookbot by reducing the number of study spaces and diminishing in size or excluding altogether a range of designated spaces. Economic factors were cited as the rationale. A return to the situation identified in mid-2021 was now on the table, although on that occasion the issues had emerged through dialogue and gradual discovery as planning proceeded. This time the news was sudden and the lack of advance notice created a real tension and compromising of trust in that vital library–estates relationship.

From a library leadership perspective, a more intense version of the independent action taken in mid-2021 needed to be mobilised, as the stakes were high, the way the project operated was on the line and time was tight. The University librarian recognised the need to take a strong stand, embrace the inevitable conflict and speak some unpopular truths to institutional leaders. This involved distancing from other project partners, addressing the University management team collectively, engaging with individual members and outlining in clear but urgent terms the reputational as well as practical consequences of reducing the capacity of the Learning Commons by a fifth. Keeping the message concise was important, and at its core was the question of whether the University would wish to be seen to have constructed the smallest main library in the Irish university sector. This question was not well received in some quarters, but its value lay in provoking a robust debate. A division of opinion was clear between those with an immediate focus on costs and those more concerned with the longer-term effectiveness of the Learning Commons as a facility for the students of tomorrow. After much debate in different fora the view of the latter group prevailed and the original capacity of $10,000\,m^2$ was agreed, a vital decision which preserved the ambition and, indeed, the integrity of the project.

Conclusion

Advancing the library building project at the University of Galway has to date extended across 25 years, with many twists and turns along the way. At the time of writing, planning permission has been secured and building design is well advanced, as is site preparation. The queue for major building projects on any campus is often long, and getting an academic library to the top of the list involves patience, persistence and politics. An estimate (Lewis, 2017) that only 10% of United States academic libraries may have been replaced or significantly renovated between 2000 and 2015 is noteworthy in this regard, highlighting that building project opportunities are rare and must be seized when they materialise. The need for lengthy advocacy should not be surprising.

Flexibility and agility have been key at the University of Galway during the past two and a half decades, along with an embracing of uncertainty at regular intervals. There has been a need to evolve the message and value proposition as well as the building concept and specification in the face of shifts in the operating environment, sometimes advantageous and sometimes unfavourable. Major changes in the construction environment, in the world at large, in higher education and on the local campus, as well as in the size and nature of the user community and its needs and expectations have shaped the Learning Commons project. When the building opens it will be unrecognisable when compared with the original concept for it in the late 1990s.

Those qualities of flexibility and agility have also been essential to how library leadership has approached the project, marked by sensitivity to key moments of opportunity and threat and a sense of preparation *for* change alongside a willingness *to* change. Engaging fully with politics and personalities, on and beyond the campus, has required constant attention, with stakeholder management an ongoing preoccupation and a valuable investment of effort which has delivered support at vital junctures. It has also been important to hold firm to the ambition and vision for the project and to fight for this, embracing conflict when necessary. A willingness to gamble occasionally, notably in delivering unpopular messages to institutional leadership or in going public with robust advocacy, has proved advantageous but could easily have turned out otherwise. Playing too safely could, however, have been equally risky, given the stakes involved, the rarity of major library building projects and the transience of moments of opportunity.

The role of luck cannot be overestimated either. This was epitomised by three key developments coinciding in 2018/19 to create the opportunity to secure government funding, as well as the good fortune that the University president had been impressed when seeing a Bookbot in action previously and therefore supported investment in this technology. Taking forward a library building project involves a huge team effort across the campus. Within the library, the backing of a committed staff has been crucial, as has a supportive structure at leadership level which has included a very helpful division of focus between the University librarian and deputy University librarian, enabling the former to concentrate on advocacy and politics. Those two areas have featured prominently in the story of this project so far and will doubtless continue to shape it. The destination is in sight, but the journey is not over yet.

References

Association of Research Libraries (2024) LibQUAL+: Charting Library Service Quality, www.libqual.org/home.

Blummer, B. and Kenton, J. M. (2017) Learning Commons in Academic Libraries: Discussing Themes in the Literature from 2001 to the Present, *New Review of Academic Librarianship*, **23**, 329–52, https://doi.org/10.1080/13614533.2017.1366925.

Cox, A. (2023) Factors Shaping Future Use and Design of Academic Library Space, *New Review of Academic Librarianship*, **29**, 33–50, https://doi.org/10.1080/13614533.2022.2039244.

Cox, A. M. and Benson-Marshall, M. (2021) Drivers for the Usage of SCONUL Member Libraries, SCONUL, www.sconul.ac.uk/knowledge-hub/space-and-design/resources-and-links.

Dematic (2016) Automated Library System: An Alternative to Conventional Shelving, https://automatedlibrarysystems.com/brochure/process.cfm#_ga=2.85302 622.651010604.1692683200-443424327.1692683200.

Gensler (2015) Libraries are for Studying, www.gensler.com/gri/students-on-libraries.

Kenny, A. (2018) Cramped, Inflexible and Uncomfortable. . . Our Students Deserve Better, *Irish Times*, 9 November, www.irishtimes.com/student-hub/cramped-inflexible-and-uncomfortable-our-students-deserve-better-1.3692127.

Lewis, D. W. (2017) Library as Place. In Gilman, T. and Lynch, B. P. (eds) *Academic Librarianship Today*, 161–76, Rowman and Littlefield.

McCaffrey, C. (2021) Planning and Implementing an Automated Storage and Retrieval System at the University of Limerick. In Atkinson, J. (ed.) *Technology, Change and the Academic Library*, 143–50, Chandos.

ODonnell, P. and Anderson, L. (2022) The University Library: Places for Possibility, *New Review of Academic Librarianship*, **28** (3), 232–55, https://doi.org/10.1080/13614533.2021.1906718.

Society of Chartered Surveyors Ireland (2024) Tender Price Index, February 2024, https://scsi.ie/wp-content/uploads/2024/02/SCSI_TenderPriceIndex_February2024-final.pdf.

Sustainable Energy Authority of Ireland (2019) Nearly Zero Energy Building Standard, www.seai.ie/business-and-public-sector/standards/nearly-zero-energy-building-standard.

University of Galway (2023) Campus Map, www.universityofgalway.ie/media/buildingsoffice/files/mapsrebranded2023/University-of-Galway-Campus_A4-Map.pdf.

9

The University of Northampton Waterside Campus

Becky Bradshaw and Chris Powis

Introduction

The University of Northampton (UON) was established as a university in 2005 and specialises in healthcare, education, science, technology, arts and business. It has approximately 12,000 students based at the main Waterside Campus and is the only university in Northamptonshire, employing around 2,200 staff, over half of whom live in the town and surrounding county.

Until 2018 the University operated from two main campuses approximately 2.5 miles apart, Park Campus just to the north of the town, and Avenue Campus, closer to the town centre.

As the name suggests, Park Campus was reminiscent of open parkland, providing an array of green space around a portfolio of academic buildings ranging in size, style, age and condition, whereas Avenue Campus comprised a variety of interconnecting buildings, many from the early 20th century, built around a series of landscaped courtyards. The campus had been recently supplemented by the purchase of an adjacent Grade II former middle school.

While distinctly different in character and design, both campuses shared similarities, and problems, associated with cost and space inefficiency. In addition, their distance from the town centre was a contributory factor to a lack of cohesion with and connection to the town and its wider population.

There was a centrally situated library on each of the old campuses. Neither was in a discrete building, but each was self-contained, with a traditional single entrance and exit arrangement guarded by library security gates. Both libraries had been extended and extensively remodelled and refurbished over the previous 20 years to accommodate growth in the physical collections, increased numbers of personal computers (PCs) and a variety of staff, study and social spaces, including a very popular library café just outside the entrance gates at Park Campus. However, growth had been largely piecemeal and opportunistic, especially at the larger Park Campus. Although both campuses were heavily used and popular with students and staff, the nature of the buildings made it difficult to articulate a coherent vision for the spaces.

Courtyards had been incorporated, walls knocked through to old studios, office and teaching spaces, and staff were scattered throughout in a variety of office designs including some carved out of study space to accommodate teams joining the library (for example, the Centre for Academic Practice) or needing space on campus (the Institute for Learning and Teaching). Only a few senior staff had individual offices.

The libraries were already modelling many of the characteristics of space and service that underpin the later design and ethos of the Learning Hub at the new campus. Space was used flexibly, with a formal and informal focus on innovation and the integration of resources, staff and space to enhance teaching and learning. Multiple teams, including academics, used the space for a range of learning and teaching interventions and were comfortable with professional service staff being integrated into their spaces and programmes. Space was managed based on trust, with few rules and regulations beyond the silent area being silent. Boundaries between social and study space were blurred, with the library café, for example, being open rather than in an enclosed space. Physical stock was still important, but an e-first acquisition policy was making significant change to provision across the board, particularly in areas like business, computing and law. Significantly too, the library was committed to collecting and responding to the student voice as expressed through major surveys like the National Student Survey (NSS), a satisfaction survey of undergraduate students in the United Kingdom and Ireland, and module surveys, as well as less formal methods like pop-up stalls around the campus to encourage students to 'vent' their frustrations or delight about the library. This gave a democratic feel to the space in that all users were heard and, where possible, their suggestions for improvement were acted upon.

Why we moved

The Browne Review (Browne, 2010) triggered major changes in the financing of higher education, and the subsequent shift to students paying more obviously for their own education meant that many now considered themselves more overtly as consumers and, as a result, student expectations increased considerably. They quite rightly expected a first-class educational experience, including high-quality teaching and learning facilities and accommodation. In Northampton we saw declining student satisfaction with the out-of-town experience, and it became increasingly clear that UON needed to respond to the changing environment and student expectation and upgrade its campus accordingly. UON needed to differentiate itself and demonstrate value for money and better facilities while ensuring adequate cost control and efficient management of the University estate.

Ultimately, the continued success of the University was dependent on our ability to recruit students and staff, and there was growing evidence that this was impacted upon by the learning and working environment on offer.

Although there was little to explicitly suggest that staff and students were unhappy on the existing campuses, the decision was made to build a completely new campus rather than renovate existing buildings. This would allow the University to rethink the idea of a campus for the 21st century and improve the quality of the facilities and space offered so as to underpin the University's future sustainability while making further efficiency savings. Key drivers for the move were:

- removal of duplication of facilities currently operating at both sites (student support services, libraries, catering and leisure facilities);
- reduction of estate management costs arising from relatively low-density campuses in two locations (more buildings mean more heating, lighting and maintenance);
- reduction in the movement of students and staff between campuses (leading to improved environmental effects and travel);
- better links with local businesses in the town centre, thereby reducing travel between campuses and the town;
- many of the existing teaching spaces (including the large, traditionally designed lecture theatres) no longer fit for purpose following a change in pedagogy to Active Blended Learning (ABL) (small group, collaborative working).

Propelled by the government's *Plan for Growth* (Department for Business, Innovation and Skills, 2011) announced in the 2011 budget, and the creation of the Northampton Waterside Enterprise Zone, the University announced plans in 2012 to develop and relocate to a new riverside campus close to Northampton town centre, publicising its vision for the newly named Waterside Campus:

Waterside will be a vibrant campus reflecting the University's values of innovation, enterprise and social impact – pioneering research and stimulating growth within Northampton and the region. This landmark development will create a modern University campus, alongside a vibrant commercial and leisure district open to the community.

(University of Northampton, n.d.)

The vision for Waterside

Through innovative design and space allocation, the new campus presented a unique opportunity to improve interaction between academic and administrative departments so as to enhance the student experience and the working environment of staff.

To break down silos, including those between professional services and the academic faculties, it was important that we did not simply replicate organisational structures and service provision through the built environment. Instead, we wanted to create buildings and spaces where multiple activities and services could reside, sharing space and giving rise to collision moments that promoted opportunities for collaboration and co-creation.

At the heart of the vision for Waterside was the idea of the 'learning commons', which at this time was a radical rethinking of academic, social and student spaces within a dynamic, fully integrated learning environment. The concept combined resources, spaces and staff from across the university in one building. Although there were examples of learning commons elsewhere in the sector, the Northampton vision extended existing thinking by including academics, much of the teaching spaces as well as front-facing professional services and resources.

A campus is made up of multiple buildings, but it was felt that the presence of a library was the most powerful signifier that it was a university. The library needed therefore to be central to the learning commons vision, an idea that survived the change of name to Learning Hub to match the other major campus building, the Creative Hub. It was this centrality to the fundamental concept of a university that dictated that the 'learning commons/hub' would not only be the most iconic building on campus, but would also be Waterside's heart. However, it would not be a stand-alone library, nor would the library service be segregated from other parts of the building or the activities within it. Instead, the library would be woven through the building design so that users were immersed in the library service, without actually stepping foot in a building named 'Library'.

It was recognised early in the project development that active interaction and involvement of library and learning professionals would improve project outcomes, avoid the potential for generic design that was unlikely to meet the strategic vision and deliver a design specifically tailored to the needs of students and staff alike. Their input would need to be active and participatory, going well beyond the traditional, passive consultation approach taken by the University for other large-scale projects.

In early 2015 the library team were asked to put down some thoughts about where the library would be positioned at Waterside. This was ostensibly to inform the architects, but it was also an opportunity to present a vision to the University management at a moment when it could potentially have traction. Rather than deliver a conventional, and probably expected, request for a new library building, albeit full of new technology and innovative learning spaces, we created a 'Day in the Life of the Learning Commons', written effectively as a film script (Powis, 2015). This hit the Zeitgeist in presenting something that was not a conventional campus building to the architects and, perhaps more importantly, the University management, including the governing body when it was presented at one of their awaydays. It caught the imagination as something that wasn't a set of demands disguised as a business plan or a dry report on floor-weighting requirements. By following University staff, students and visitors as they entered and used the building over the course of a day it gave flesh to what was then an abstract idea of a campus. The first paragraph sets the scene and tone:

> It's 8.30 and first year history student Alice sleepwalks through the glass door into the foyer. Her university smartcard in her bag is picked up by sensors but all she cares about is a caffeine and sugar hit from the cafe. This is the best coffee on campus and has added 'virtue' from being a social enterprise. She takes her coffee and pastry to one of the tables with good sight lines to the entrance and waits for her friends to arrive. They have a presentation later this morning and want a final run through. She checks the university's iNorthampton app and sees that a couple of them have already communicated some updates. It also shows that they're all pretty close to uni so she'd better wake up!

And the story continues through other students and academics. For example:

> The presentation is tweaked and automatically saved to the shared area and Alice's group leave for their class in a room on the first floor. As they cross the foyer she sees Martin, her personal tutor. He waves and continues into the building. Martin has a meeting with the Learning Technologists and is looking forward to trying out the latest immersive technology space. After this morning's induction he'll bring his third years back as he is hoping to use it to simulate the battle of Waterloo. This is also part of his Napoleonic history MOOC and he is working with the Learning Techs to upload it for his thousands of students to work with.

It includes external visitors and ends with a visit by the local business community:

Those that haven't visited before are impressed with the building – it certainly has a 'wow' factor but it also has a timeless quality. This will be a building that people will use to identify Northampton far into the future. The CEO of Avon comments on how the sight lines are constantly surprising as they reveal wide open spaces from some angles, and quirky, almost eccentric areas from another. It is obvious where the key things are – books, self-service issue etc., but there is a real incentive to explore the space too.

Although it was clearly at times fanciful, it became an influential document for the ultimate design of the building, cementing the head of Library and Learning Services into the main campus planning groups and committees and ensuring that the library head's voice was important to our architects, MCW, who actively listened and engaged with his vision. Although we were not intending to build a library as such, the library 'voice' might not have carried the same weight during campus planning without the 'Day in the Life' document.

It could be said UON had taken a co-operative approach to the Learning Hub development well before 'co-design' became the buzzword it is today, with the approach embedded into the project structure very early in development. Active engagement and co-creation included library and learning professionals taking an equal part in the design process, being part of the project and design team and contributing to and shaping discussion in workshops, design team meetings, research visits and client-side meetings. Ultimately, they were involved in all key decisions on design, development and operation.

A pedagogic shift too

There were, as described above, changes to the way we worked, and especially in the way that we delivered learning and teaching that pre-dated the move but were crucial to the design of the campus.

However, the change that is most associated with Waterside is the change to a new pedagogy for Northampton – Active Blended Learning (ABL). This is expressed as follows at Northampton:

[S]tudents learn in small groups and through close interaction between staff and students. Our courses are designed for active learning on and off campus, in digitally rich environments that integrate 'live', real-time sessions with activities students can undertake where they like and at the time they choose.

(University of Northampton, 2021)

This approach was introduced by Professor Ale Armellini, the then dean of the Institute of Learning and Teaching, in 2015. The intention was to adopt this approach regardless of the move to Waterside. However, once the move was confirmed, the physical requirements for learning and teaching became central to the plans. This was often, wrongly, characterised as no lectures, and therefore no need for large lecture theatres. A lecture can be an excellent way of delivering knowledge and, as such, remains in the academic toolkit at Northampton. Lectures can also be active and include blended elements, so they fit into ABL.

ABL had early adopters and champions in the faculties and among those delivering information, digital and academic skills in professional services. It was difficult to fully embed as normal practice across the institution when the campuses still had spaces that encouraged the large-scale transmission of information to tiered rows of students. However, a team of learning designers led by the dean of Learning and Teaching worked with academics to self-assess their ABL status before the move. Nearly all declared that they had adapted their courses to enable delivery by ABL at the point of the move.

It is difficult to quantify how many staff left the University because of the move to Waterside, including the change to ABL. Anecdotally, several academics left because of the change to ABL or the move away from offices or both. Turnover of professional services staff was higher at the end of COVID-19 than in the first 18 months of the opening of the new campus, but insight from staff exit surveys indicated that this was more influenced by a reappraisal of work–life balance than negativity towards a return to Waterside.

We have now moved to depoliticise ABL by removing the capital letters and to further embed active, blended learning as our default pedagogy rather than as a project linked to the campus. The campus was built around the pedagogy, but the emphasis on ABL rather than what it stood for was very much seen as part of the move. We have now moved beyond this. It also enables us to better develop active, blended delivery that recognises prior learner experience and subject, and to level differences.

The basic principles of active, blended learning haven't therefore changed in the five years since the move. The definition of ABL quoted above pre-dates the move and is still relevant. There are still no lecture theatres on Waterside campus, although a couple of new large teaching spaces have been created to allow for team-based learning and, for example, large group inductions. Some academics still occasionally lecture to small groups as part of a module but will still include small-scale activities as part of a more didactic session.

Despite undertaking substantial research, we have little real evidence that ABL has impacted on student continuation, progression or achievement either positively or negatively (Wareing, 2021). The metrics show that where there is excellent teaching, good assessment practice and academic support, then students achieve their potential. There are no significant differences in how ABL is perceived between different protected characteristics or between international students and home students. There has also been little obvious change in the way the buildings are used from the old campuses. There is some evidence that the approach is popular with prospective students, especially the emphasis on small group teaching.

We designed the campus around the student experience and around a pedagogy that emphasised small group, active and in-person teaching integrated with blended, online interventions, resources and activities. It would be difficult to reverse this and rebuild to accommodate large group in-person teaching on campus. We coped well during COVID-19, largely because the infrastructure and skill set of students and staff were there to enable the pivot to remote teaching. But we are a campus-based university and the return to in-person teaching was welcomed by the majority of students and staff. ABL enables us to retain the best elements of the campus and virtual learning environments.

The transition to agile or smart working and the move to ABL meant that UON coped relatively well during the COVID-19 pandemic. The return to campus working also allowed us to learn from the close-down and rationalise workspaces even further. This included refining team-based working agreements, remote vs on-campus expectation, and co-location of other professional service departments in the Learning Hub.

How did we engage with stakeholders?

Engagement took a three-pronged approach: university-wide, departmental/ faculty and external. The University and the library teams consulted with a range of stakeholders including staff, students and relevant external users or bodies, while external consultation included visits, meetings and research with other universities and university libraries.

The main University consultations took the form of exhibitions and staff and student meetings. These were open and/or structured, topic-specific sessions and used a variety of formats, including online, face-to-face, opportunities for anonymous feedback and meetings and exhibitions showcasing, for example, plans, models and furniture choices. This was also a chance for the 'red lines' associated with the project to be aired and understood. These came from the top and included controversial issues like the demise of faculty buildings, hotdesking and parking.

There was also an expectation, not always uniformly delivered across the University, that members of steering groups and campus planning meetings would act in part as representatives, and trickle down information to their areas. However, the avoidance of hard issues, especially around the 'red lines', led to more difficult conversations, especially within the faculties, closer to the move. The library team deliberately set out to avoid this scenario, however, and all staff were kept informed from an early stage. Work streams were created early on, for example on shelving or stock weeding, involving staff at all levels in preparation for the move. Plans were displayed in common rooms and regular updates were provided in a weekly staff e-mail and during termly open meetings.

The library took part in the University all-staff consultation, including specific meetings on what the library service would look like at Waterside, or were part of wider meetings on resources and infrastructure. These were, for the most part, well attended but could easily be hijacked by personal concerns, for example on where academics could keep their personal copies of texts. We also hosted the main exhibition space in the library foyer which contained models of the campus and mock-ups of a student room.

One problem with a completely new campus was that all but a very few could access the site as the campus took shape. There were virtual and, latterly, photographic fly-throughs, some viewings arranged from the roof of a nearby building and architect's maps and drawings, but it was still difficult to make sense of what the buildings looked like and how they would work in practice. This made it important for the ways of working to be modelled at the old campuses, and the vice chancellor very visibly started agile working by giving up his office. There were also small-scale structural changes to spaces that, prior to the moves to Waterside and ABL, inevitably changed some teaching spaces.

We undertook consultation with students on their experience of using the libraries at the old campuses and what they would like to see retained, changed and improved, given a clean slate. We used vox pops, informal interviews and informal chats, but our main route was through a project that followed a representative group of undergraduate students, recruited two years before the move, throughout their time at the University, thus including two years at the old campuses and one year at Waterside.

The involvement of students was difficult because, until quite late in the project, most of those approached informally for their thoughts on the development of the new library space would not be going to the new campus, and it was therefore difficult to engage them. This was unfortunate because the big decisions were made relatively early on, and by the time we talked to those students who were going, it was more to do with selling the move rather than receiving feedback that could influence anything much beyond things such as furniture. Although central communications to students were well planned and delivered, most indicated that they got information on the new campus via gossip rather than official sources. Although most thought we were building a traditional library, others had 'heard' that we were not having physical books at all.

The more formal project with students straddling the move was more interesting. In their first year, two years before the move, most were disinterested. It simply seemed too far ahead, and they were more concerned with establishing themselves as students. In their second year they were more willing to express opinions on how the new campus should work, but after the move, in their final year, they were again more interested in finishing their course and getting a job than commenting much beyond how they liked the environment.

The semi-structured interviews did throw up some useful themes, however. Perhaps most important to us was that the word 'library', although widely understood and liked as a concept, was not something that they needed on a building. We included the library resources and services in a Learning Hub and students were happy to accept this. They were also not at all concerned with the integration of library spaces and services with other social and academic spaces. One student summed up for the group by saying that they just wanted what they needed at the time when they needed it, and they didn't care what the buildings were called. We were worried that not having a library building would detract from the perception of the campus as an academic space, but this was not a concern of the students at the time and has not featured in feedback since.

There was also widespread support for eclectic and even eccentric spaces. The old libraries had these in abundance, due to the organic way in which they had expanded, and these were widely praised. Expanding these spaces at Waterside became part of the space planning, especially for the Learning Hub.

Consultation about the move also took the form of visits to universities and libraries in Europe (Finland and the Netherlands), the United States (especially the University of North Carolina) and closer to home, like Oxford Brookes and Canterbury Christ Church. These provided great insight and we are grateful for the honesty and hospitality shown to us by all.

Estates strategy/vision

As previously outlined, the project brief included the desire to break down barriers between individual departments and faculties and remove the silo approach to campus planning which had resulted in many campuses, including our own, being developed in piecemeal fashion with individual properties designed with their owners such as 'business school' or 'library' in mind. This shift allowed the new campus to be arranged by typology of space, paving the way for the fundamental shift from spaces 'owned' by faculties and departments to space 'shared' by all stakeholders.

Interdepartmental and faculty collaboration and community development was to be encouraged through fusion facilities, with shared working spaces for all staff groups and activity-based working environments, achieved through flexible and efficient furniture design and placement. Bright and well-designed open-plan workspaces replaced all individual offices, and both academic and professional service staff were encouraged and empowered to work anywhere on campus, choosing their work location in accordance with the task or activity being performed. In the main, workstations were no longer assigned to individuals, and the workstation-to-person ratio was reduced substantially. Yet finding an available desk was not a problem, with many choosing to work in 'touch down' locations or spaces which would traditionally be reserved for students, including shared social spaces. Six years on, this behaviour is observed. All buildings at Waterside offer this mix of task-orientated spaces to be shared by all users, but, with the blend of teaching, working, learning and social spaces in the Learning Hub, it quickly became the most popular environment on campus.

It was, of course, necessary to provide some segregation between staff and students, and so academic workspaces were carefully incorporated into the Learning Hub design to directly support the learning needs of students and encourage cross-disciplinary collaboration, while also allowing for uninterrupted work where necessary. However, staff were encouraged to make the most of the Learning Hub environment and not to shut themselves away from students and colleagues.

The move to shared, ownerless workspaces meant priority needed to be given to the uniformity and ergonomic design of furniture and equipment so as to ensure maximum usability by staff. High-quality operator chairs with maximum adjustability were introduced alongside standard workstation configurations with an increased proportion of sit–stand options to allow flexibility for the user, even where standardisation was required.

A substantial change, initiated by the smarter working approach and shift to shared workspaces from individual offices or desks, was the move to a paper-light environment. A project to reduce reliance on printed materials commenced with the launch of digital document storage and an army of industrial-sized scanners. Supported by estates project managers, library staff were early adopters of the paper-light approach, working with colleagues to digitise records and minimise unnecessary document storage solutions in a project originally named the De-Clutter Project. This approach, coupled with a need to reduce the shelving footprint, meant a reduction of around 43% in the print collections. Working with academics, titles that were on reading lists were replaced, where possible, with e-versions and a data-driven approach was taken to assessing the appropriateness, relevance and usage of print titles. The result is a much harder-working and more relevant print collection.

In addition to large-scale fundamental change, the move to Waterside and a new way of working brought with it additional changes that, while small, risked greater impact than primary changes such as the move to open-plan workspaces or smarter working. These changes related primarily to comfort and environment, ergo reflecting physiological requirement akin to Maslow's lower level in the hierarchy of needs (Maslow, 1943). Sweating the small stuff became important and small working groups were formed to explore how refreshments would be provided in the absence of team members paying into tea kitties (in the end, the university provided free tea, coffee, milk and sugar out of the central budget), equipment and personal effects would be stored safely while individuals moved from building to building (banks of keypad-operated, single-use day lockers were introduced throughout the building) and the age-old argument about who last used the microwave without cleaning it would be addressed. Similar small-scale environmental changes designed to provide comfort to the user extended to the learning, library and self-study spaces that permeate the Learning Hub building, where comfort, variety and integrated power through mains and USB (universal serial bus) supply take priority. Individual booths and enclosed units which cocoon the user were introduced and remain the most popular furniture choice of both students and staff.

This new environment and way of working or learning brought with it a need to review standard operational facilities or estates practices, such as the introduction of flow cleaning (cleaning teams deployed to perform specific tasks) throughout the campus, and much greater onus on the estates and campus services and IT (information technology) services to identify and remedy faults proactively, given that the shared space approach meant that no particular team took responsibility for logging or monitoring helpdesk requests. A specific working group, reporting directly to the overarching project board, focused on operational readiness to assist with this transition, addressing requirements such as these, but it was not easy. The group formed approximately three years prior to the opening of the new campus so as to enable operational input into design and get a head start on the transformational change that was required in these departments. However, it was very difficult for operational teams to design an operating model for a new building (and campus) they could not see, especially when it was so vastly different to the campus they were currently supporting; the parameters changed regularly due to changes to the design brief, or the external landscape influenced the internal design environment. As an example, the Learning Hub was originally designed, and was being built, with very little by way of security controls in place. However, the tragic Manchester arena bombing in May 2017 initiated a fundamental review of security measures throughout the building and campus, leading to the introduction of access-control and speed-lane gates less than nine months prior to opening. Despite the planning that took place in the early stages, much of the operational readiness, including the introduction of new staffing structures and working patterns, took place in the last 18 months, due to changes such as these.

How did the Learning Hub and the library within work in practice?
Guiding principles
The Learning Hub, and to a large extent the campus, is built around four guiding principles: adaptable, integrated, IT-rich and democratic. The library sits within the Learning Hub and, therefore, the space and service are underpinned by those principles. By following them we challenged a number of sectoral and professional shibboleths, especially around the provision of PCs, security and behaviour.

We see the space as adaptable rather than flexible. The latter implies that it would be reset after a short-term change and, although this is certainly the case in some circumstances, it is also true that space use has changed quickly in response to need. The shelving is fixed in particular parts of each floor through floor weighting, but virtually all of the other spaces can be changed easily by staff or students to facilitate social, academic or study uses. Much of the furniture is moveable, and the general teaching spaces are minimalist in design so that use defines layout rather than being enforced by it. Some spaces did not work as intended and were changed with limited disruption; for example, a coffee shop is now the home of Counselling and Mental Health and ASSIST (disability support), but the ethos of adapting the environment to the immediate needs of the user remains a practical reality.

There was a feeling among some, mainly academic staff, that a campus needs named buildings such as a library or a business school. These staff members believed that to not have these buildings would confuse and dissuade prospective students, parents and investors that we are a serious university. However, this has not been borne out in practice. We have impressive buildings that are built around learning and teaching and student experience rather than university power structures, and this impresses applicants and external stakeholders. The space is adaptable enough to be a library when you want it to be, but also a teaching, meeting, social or study space too. A campus needs something that looks and works like a library to signal learning and function for its users, but it doesn't have to be in a separate building and be called a library. The Learning Hub is somewhere that inspires earnest study and gives a focus to work, study and social interaction and therefore serves as, and is widely accepted as and often called, the library.

However, it is true that questions have been raised, especially by academics, around the loss of identity and belonging through shared space. Lab- and studio-based subjects still do have specialist spaces that the students and staff can readily identify with, but students in other subjects tend to congregate around particular areas of the Learning Hub anyway. Sometimes this is because their physical resources are in that area or because they are mainly taught on that floor. Sometimes it is because the area is conducive to the way they learn or need to work. Zoning or explicit labelling of areas in the building may implicitly exclude some students. Students have made the building work for them by creating their own spaces within it based on their needs at any given time. The building allows them to define how they wish to 'belong' rather than forcing them into faculty or university definitions.

Students and staff find their own space or favourite table or chair. This is true in any building, but especially in libraries. The spaces are adaptable enough to move furniture and we have eclectic and sometimes eccentric spaces to use across the Learning Hub and the campus, but most people can find somewhere that they are comfortable and happy without being signposted towards it.

To achieve this adaptability, we made one of the biggest and most significant student-facing decisions in not providing fixed open PCs. Waterside is a Bring Your Own Device (BYOD) campus; although there are computer labs, these are usually closed to all but those students needing specialist software or high-spec hardware for their course. We do offer all home undergraduate students a laptop on enrolment and supplement this with around 350 laptops for loan, but it was a high-risk strategy to move overnight from masses of open-access PCs situated in IT centres, the libraries, labs and other spaces on the old campus to none. This went against the sector norm, where it was seen as unchallengeable that students wanted and needed more open access PCs.

However, feedback of any sort was virtually non-existent on the change; for example, the first NSS after the move mentioned PCs just seven times, and the change freed library and IT staff from constant maintenance of PCs and PC areas. It isn't perfect, and some, especially international students, do arrive with very old or underpowered hardware. This is why we retained laptops for loan.

Although we could not have known it at the time of the move, the BYOD policy supported by the laptop offer meant that we could be reasonably sure that students had the basic equipment to cope with remote teaching during COVID-19. We still had to work on supporting Wi-Fi via the provision of dongles in home settings where possible and helping with the digital skills of some students, although most were generally able to cope with the change.

A new footprint

The new campus had a smaller footprint overall than the old campuses and we did not want to compromise adaptability by taking a large legacy print collection. We had had a clear and accepted e-first purchasing policy for some years, although it is important to note that this was not an e-only policy. However, moving required us to reduce the print collection by over 40% and this was achieved in the two years leading up to the move. We expected resistance from some students and subject groups, but this did not materialise to any extent. Some subjects work better in print (children's books, art) and we do still buy print in these and other subjects. However, we replaced books on reading lists with e-copies where possible, while offering a more limited number of print titles to supplement the online copies. It is true that some students and academics prefer print, but the feedback is generally positive, with the NSS and other surveys practically free of calls for more copies of titles.

The space is IT rich. It had to be when our pedagogic approach of ABL and 80% of library resources being online meant that students needed to connect seamlessly to reliable and powerful Wi-Fi within the classrooms as well as in their study and social contexts. This aspect was not without problems. For the first year or so of occupation the Wi-Fi was not able to cope and the classroom technology was flaky, leading to considerable frustration from staff and students that was reflected in the major student surveys. Wi-Fi is now as important as ensuring that water comes out of the taps and, although changes were implemented, including a separate network for gamers and more and better-placed nodes, the memory of the first months cast a long shadow that has not fully left us yet.

The integrated nature of the building meant that solutions to the traditional library security concerns around stock management, such as staffed exit points, were not implemented. There are multiple access and egress points in a large and complex 24/7 building. None of those exits are staffed, although all have library security gates. These monitor which books are leaving the building and whether they have gone through the self-service machines, but they do not stop anyone exiting. This led to fears that most print stock would disappear, but although it is true that many books are taken out informally, it is equally true that many of them are subsequently returned. Access to the special collection is mediated, but giving up the security of stock to allow wider access to the other spaces and uses of the building was difficult for library staff. Trust is at the heart of the way the building is managed, however, and it must be accepted that trust will sometimes be abused.

Space ownership

The lack of ownership also led to fears that the building would turn into a lawless space with little or no control over its users. Bad behaviour from some students had been an issue in the old libraries, but we have noticed a significant improvement since moving to Waterside. This may be down to the attractiveness of the new buildings or the integration of teaching and, especially, academic staff into the new spaces.

The lack of confidential working space in the staff areas was also questioned before the move. However, there are plenty of bookable or ad hoc private spaces in rooms or booths that allow for confidential conversations or work on sensitive documents. Flexible working, especially after COVID-19, means that concentrated work can be arranged around home working or undertaken in the silent area of the Learning Hub. Staff use of the open spaces has the bonus of modelling academic or working practices to students.

There were fears that no one would ever know where anyone was if they did not have their own offices. This assumes that we knew this before the move, which was not true. We remain territorial beings and tend to stay in roughly the same area within the open offices. Integrating space was intended to increase collaboration between teams, leading to better understanding of the challenges faced by other professional services or even to the development of innovative new courses as academics mingled across their subject divide. Collaboration has improved, although perhaps not as much in the academic sphere. It is easier to deliberately or accidentally meet staff in the Learning Hub, sparking productive conversations and often finding solutions to issues that may have taken much more organising in the more distributed pre-Waterside campuses.

However, it is worth noting that work undertaken before the move found occupancy of academic workspaces at around 38%, whereas in the first year after the move it was 32%. COVID-19 has disrupted this further for academic and professional services staff, but effective use of MS Outlook calendars and 'office hours' have mitigated the impact.

The space is democratic in that no one owns any spaces and no one, therefore, has exclusive use of or responsibility for spaces apart from a few specialist teaching rooms. All spaces are managed by Estates and Campus Services, freeing staff in the library from the tyranny of day-to-day space management. This change was popular with managers across the University but, as described, did require an approach that Estates and Campus Services, and IT to some extent, were not familiar with. The building operates 24/7, 365 days a year and is kept open and appropriately staffed centrally. Anyone can suggest amended use of space within the Learning Hub, but decisions are then made in a more collegiate way than when buildings were owned and considered as power blocs to represent an individual's or faculty's power and influence. This included the library, which led to duplication of, for example, social learning spaces in different buildings that were little used in practice. The most well-resourced areas of the University no longer have the most well-resourced spaces, as all space is of the highest quality. This doesn't take away from professional expertise in managing space; for example, decisions about shelving would still be led by library staff. It does mean that more people are involved in decisions that impact on them directly. This change, although radical in nature, has been relatively uncontested and, where challenged, has been managed sensitively and towards mutually acceptable solutions.

It is important to note, however, that unless they are presented with alternative visions many people will not be able to articulate what they want in a campus, other than to say more of what they like. Sometimes we need to trust our expertise, experience and vision and be brave enough to present options that push boundaries. Most things can be amended and will evolve anyway so that students and staff are challenged to imagine a different way of working.

Conclusion

It is unlikely that UON will develop another property on the campus with similar attributes to the Learning Hub in the near future. However, any future campus development will replicate the successful approach to co-design used throughout this development. The co-creation of the Learning Hub with the library was perhaps the best example of collaboration in practice.

In the early days of post-completion, a 'Learning Hub Operations' group was established for colleagues to come together to discuss management of the building and spaces within it. The group quickly became redundant, as the ethos and approach to space use and lack of ownership were readily accepted by stakeholders. This remains true five years later.

The Learning Hub works. Very little has changed from the original design and concept, and such change as has occurred has been because of services wishing to be part of the vibrant, connected and collaborative environment that the Learning Hub offers. Our postgraduate research community, Students' Union officers and Student Futures team have all recently relocated, citing the Learning Hub as the heart of the campus. Of course, there are areas where we will need to resolve different perspectives on issues like ownership of space, especially when new staff join the university. Internal pressure on spaces, exacerbated by the growing need for new specialised teaching rooms, have meant that some spaces have been repurposed. Although individuals can, to some extent, control their personal environments – for example, through ventilation or specialised equipment – supporting the needs of neurodiverse staff and students still presents challenges that we are working through. Managed student access to academics when they are in staff-only spaces has also presented challenges that have been reflected in student feedback. We will need to find solutions that work for both parties. On a smaller scale, extra power points have been installed and some of the larger, fixed furniture has been reconfigured. However, the building and design remain, in essence, untouched, suggesting that the approach taken to co-design was indeed effective. The Learning Hub and the wider campus will continue to evolve but that evolution has remained, and will remain, true to the original concepts of adaptability, integration and democracy enabled, but not driven, by technology.

References

Browne, Lord Browne of Madingley (2010) Securing a Sustainable Future for Higher Education: An Independent Review of Higher Education Funding and Student Finance, www.independent.gov.uk/browne-report.

Department for Business, Innovation and Skills (2011) The Plan for Growth, https://assets.publishing.service.gov.uk/media/5a7cb81e40f0b6629523b637/2011budget_growth.pdf.

Maslow, A. H. (1943) A Theory of Human Motivation, *Psychological Review*, **50** (4), 370–96.

Powis, C. (2015) A Day in the Life of the Learning Commons. Unpublished.

University of Northampton (2021) Introducing Active Blended Learning, https://mypad.northampton.ac.uk/lte/2021/10/29/active-blended-learning-abl.

University of Northampton (n.d.) A Vision for Waterside: UON Strategic Brief. Unpublished.

Wareing, S. (2021) Measuring the Success of Active Blended Learning. In Padilla Rodriquez, B. C. and Armellini, A. (eds) *Cases on Active Blended Learning in Higher Education*, IGI Global.

10

Social and Informal Learning Spaces and Inclusion

Andrew Cox, Melanie Benson Marshall,
Jennifer A. Burnham, Leo Care, Chris Clow,
Savannah Hanson, Tim Herrick, Myles Jones
and Alison Little

Introduction

> Space – whether physical or virtual, individual or shared – can have an important impact on learning. It can bring people together; it can encourage exploration, collaboration and discussion; it can also frame an unspoken message of exclusion, disconnectedness and disengagement.

(Elkington, 2019, 3)

As pedagogy has moved away from knowledge transmission through lectures to more independent forms of learning and group work, recognition of the importance of social and informal learning spaces on campuses has risen (Bennett, 2009; Cox and Benson Marshall, 2021). Students need places to study, and often their residential accommodation is not well designed to support this. Acknowledging the importance of physical spaces is also to recognise the physical and emotional dimensions of learning (Cox, 2017). While digital might have been thought to reduce the importance of space, in fact we know that the digital has a strong material dimension (Gourlay and Oliver, 2018). Devices are physical objects that need to be carried, handled and charged, and their role in learning is shaped by the physical and social contexts of their use. And while digital has reduced the need for libraries to be warehouses for books, it has opened up the potential for libraries to offer multiple types of space to support different forms of learning. Librarians have demonstrated growing wisdom about how to design library spaces that enable learning. This has given them a potentially influential role in reconceptualising university space as a whole. How libraries have been redesigned provides a model for reconfiguring the whole estate to be much more about supporting different types of learning, rather than seeing the lecture theatre as the only place where learning happens or focusing on the material environment and not on the feel of spaces.

Thus, understanding how to create better social and informal learning spaces has grown in importance (Sodexo, 2022). Another significant driver of change in universities has been that with the widening of participation in higher education (HE) there has been a need for universities to evolve to ensure equality, diversity and inclusion (EDI). Design of campus space has a role here too, because campus design both shapes learning practices and makes symbolic statements about the character of academic institutions. Estates strategy must be more than about providing efficient or even environmentally sustainable infrastructure, but through its design must promote inclusivity. So, it has become more important to investigate what makes good social and informal learning spaces, and part of this is to discover what different needs there are across the diverse student community.

This chapter describes one of our studies at the University of Sheffield exploring what qualities students want from social and informal learning spaces and what is needed to ensure inclusivity in the design of such spaces.

Literature review

While the importance of campus as a space and place is recognised in the literature of education, there has been a relative neglect of study of informal learning spaces. An exception to this is the library literature, which is rich with examples of the development of different types of space needed for independent and group study. Authors such as Scott Bennett have been influential in reflecting on how the paradigm of library space design has shifted from book centred to learning centred (Bennett, 2009). One of the defining features of the information and learning commons is an emphasis on variety of spaces (Watson, 2007). The library literature tells us a lot about the different types of spaces that students use, but there does seem to be a gap in terms of investigating how different communities of students might experience the spaces differently (Cox and Benson Marshall, 2021). In the last few years there has been a growth in concern for ensuring EDI in all aspects of university life, including learning. The widening of participation in higher education makes this essential. Space designs based on a norm of a student who is young, white, male, working 9 am to 5 pm and non-disabled have to be increasingly challenged.

It has long been recognised that campus design plays a part in projecting particular views of learning which may make it less accessible to minoritised groups. For example, how spaces are designed and furnished sends unconscious messages that make students from working-class backgrounds feel less welcomed and comfortable, as a form of invisible curriculum (Costello, 2002; Gair and Mullins, 2002; Tor, 2015). Such research often suggests that the library is perceived to be a place which is less culturally exclusive than other parts of campus, but we should be alert to shifting expectations (Soria, 2013).

An important dimension of inclusion is for people with minoritised sexual and gender identities. Research shows that campuses are not experienced as entirely safe by LGBTQ+ students. They often experience discrimination or verbal abuse, chiefly from other students, in places such as the students' union building or halls of residence (Ellis, 2009). As a result, students often feel that they have to mask expressions of their identity so as to ensure their safety on campus. One study refers to an ambivalent sense of students feeling 'safe but unsafe' because of contradictions in messaging; for example, posters against discrimination are contradicted by the lack of gender-neutral toilets (Allen et al., 2020). In other research LGBTQ+ students felt invisible in a bad way because their community was not acknowledged in official representations of the student body, but also visible in a bad way because of experiences of microaggressions. In a campus context where these feelings of ambivalence abound, evidence suggests that libraries are experienced as quiet, safe spaces which are particularly valued. The library is also seen as a place to find out information safely about LGBTQ+ issues, although there is always room for improvement in terms of offering access to such information (Stewart and Kendrick, 2019; Wexelbaum, 2018).

Disabled students may also have problematic experiences on campus. What might appear to be a 'neutral' design to a non-disabled person can be experienced very differently by those with some form of disability. Library lighting, acoustics, cleanliness and signage can all have a strong impact on those with particular disabilities (Pionke, 2017). Pionke (2017) found that students with disabilities place a high priority on quiet spaces to study, lockers and easier physical access. It is felt to be symbolic of marginalisation if disabled access is via a side entrance, as is commonly the case. The location of the library can itself have an impact on shaping its accessibility (Pontoriero and Zippo-Mazur, 2019).

This and other aspects of EDI are shifting agendas. The range of disabilities that are recognised is widening. Earlier emphasis was on physical issues, such as those affecting physical movement or sensory disabilities, like poor sight. Increasingly, the range of recognised neurodiversity is widening. People on the autistic spectrum can have very different experiences of spaces (Andrews, 2016; Shea and Derry, 2019) and there is increasing recognition of the needs of neurodiverse students (Hamilton and Petty, 2023; Shaw and Selman, 2023). Sensory issues are central to their experience of university life, such as student accommodation, and so issues around design and use of space remain important. Yet such disability is invisible (Andrews, 2016). Issues of mental health are now also considered a form of disability. To be welcoming, the informal learning spaces should ideally be designed with consideration (and participation) of all these communities.

Libraries have a tradition of seeking to be inclusive towards disabilities (Jaeger, 2018), but our understanding of the underlying issues has shifted (Hamraie, 2016). At one time disability was seen as an individual problem requiring rehabilitation. In the 1980s a social model of disability showed that inaccessibility in the built environment was the problem, not the individual. Building on this, universal design was seen as offering principles that could accommodate the needs of all. However, critical disability theory goes further in seeing differing abilities as having their own value as a way of experiencing the world rather than as something to be cured or rehabilitated. In this view, universal design is unhelpful in tending to decentre disability, and because it focuses on technical issues rather than acknowledging that discrimination is created through power.

The aspect of inclusivity that has been shifted most in recent years is around race and ethnicity. We know that there is a persistent gap in entry to university and attainment experienced by students from ethnic minorities (Stevenson et al., 2019). Acknowledgment of the problem on campuses of inclusion of ethnic minorities has strengthened with the Black Lives Matter movement, resonating with calls to decolonise the curriculum. Whereas earlier research suggested that the campus, and the library in particular, were seen by Black, Asian and Minority Ethnic (BAME) students as safe spaces (Whitmire et al., 2011), feelings have shifted because of growing self-awareness and a more robust willingness of students to confront all forms of discrimination. Evidence such as the Halpin (2022) report on experiences in student accommodation points to the many difficult experiences Black students have at university; more than half had experienced racism, nearly two-thirds witnessed it. Samatar et al. (2021) capture some very difficult experiences of non-identification with the university, expressed by feeling deeply uncomfortable in campus spaces. The implications for design of informal and social learning spaces are challenging (Beilin, 2017; Brook et al., 2015). Aspects of decor – such as references to benefactors – can be experienced as micro-aggressions (Brook et al., 2015). Decor can project spaces where white is the norm (Santamaria, 2020), and students can feel alienated if they do not see people like themselves or their culture represented in spaces (Broughton, 2019; Harwood et al., 2018). Decolonisation challenges imperial resonances in western architecture and the content and classification systems used for library collections. Campus spaces occupied by people behaving in typical, 'white' student ways are experienced as alienating (Broughton, 2019; Harwood et al., 2018).

The campus is often seen as safer than the wider city environment, and to contain truly safe, 'counter spaces'. However, it can also feel like 'contradictory space' because of conflicting messages and also to contain spaces that are white, heteronormative, ableist 'fortified spaces' (Harwood et al., 2018). Libraries have often, in past research, been found to be counter spaces, but we must increasingly recognise limits on this. The claim that the library is a 'neutral' space may disguise that it is neutral only from a privileged, white, male, Global North perspective. Our research sought to discover how these issues were being successfully addressed in the context of our own campus.

Research method

The study on which this chapter is based sought to more fully understand students' experiences of informal and social learning spaces across the campus, building on previous work about students' use of study space (Cox et al., 2022). We began by conducting four focus groups with a total of 14 participants (plus two student facilitators) in April 2022. The focus groups explored students' experiences of the campus, where they liked to study, and also asked participants whether they felt campus spaces were inclusive. The focus groups were followed by a questionnaire which was distributed in July 2022 and which received 179 responses. The invitation to participate emphasised our desire to gain responses from minoritised communities. The survey had two main parts: the first asked participants 'What is your favourite study space and why?' From this we sought to identify both the most favoured spaces and the factors lying behind the choice. The second part of the questionnaire included a number of questions to discover students' feelings of inclusivity. One question asked whether the respondent identified as 'BAME', 'a person with a disability', 'LGBTQ+', 'from a working class background', 'an international student', 'having strong religious beliefs' or 'someone with dependents or major caring responsibilities'. We used this terminology on the advice of the Students' Union but understood that these are terms that are themselves open to multiple interpretation and contestation. In a survey it is hard to fully account for such important differences of interpretation. At the time of undertaking the study we were advised that 'BAME' and 'person with a disability' were the most suitable terms; now we would probably not use those terms, reflecting changing perceptions and language even within a short time frame. We then asked participants if they felt their choice of study space was linked to any of these identities and, if so, how. We also asked 'Are there spaces you would like to study in, but you don't feel they are inclusive? If so, what makes you feel they are not inclusive?'

Findings
What students want from social and informal learning spaces

In the survey students identified their favourite places to study. The University libraries featured prominently in the list, including:

- the traditional book-centric Western Bank Library;
- the Information Commons (IC) building, with its diverse study spaces, computers and selective book collections;
- the new Diamond building. Ostensibly for the engineering faculty, with labs, the Diamond also has a large number of independent study spaces of different types with a variety of types of furnishing, as well as a library area and a makerspace.

Other important study places were the Students' Union and home.

Analysis of the reasons given for choices in the focus groups and the explanation of preferred spaces in the questionnaire produced a list of 13 interconnected criteria that students often mentioned as important to them in choosing a space to study. Students' preferences differ; for example, there is a definite divide between preferences for completely silent focus and those who just want relative quiet. While each student might mention only a few of the factors, all the factors were mentioned many times by different students, so they offer a guide to what shapes preferences. Here we present the list of 13 factors as one of the main findings of the study, followed by summarisation of the responses.

1 **Welcoming:** Is there a sense of belonging, be that as a University of Sheffield student or relative to the student's faculty or department? Do the decor and activities happening in the building suggest that it is a space where they are welcome?
2 **Easy to find and navigate:** Is it easy to way-find in the building and understand how a space is allowed to be used? Is there information about times the room will be available for use?
3 **Walkable and convenient:** Is the building and its study space within a few minutes' walk or a natural route from where the student has been doing other things, such as having lectures or accommodation? Are the times the buildings are open suitable?
4 **Suitable for the task:** Is the study space suitable for the task in hand, such as concentrated revision versus more low-pressure background research or answering e-mails?
5 **Social:** Is the student able to work alongside or stay in contact with friends, and perhaps do group work?

6 **Studious:** Are study spaces clearly signalled as being for study by appropriate signage, by decoration and furnishing, and by what others are doing?

7 **Connected and resourced:** Does the building offer spaces with good connectivity (e.g., Wi-Fi, device-charging points, etc.)? Are computers available? Are appropriate books and other study resources available?

8 **Flexible:** Can one use the space flexibly (e.g., furniture can be re-arranged; one can eat, drink, talk, work, sit, move around as one needs)?

9 **Safe:** Do the building and its spaces feel secure (e.g., can one leave possessions there, within reason; the individual feels personally safe)?

10 **Quiet:** Are noise levels appropriate for how the individual likes to study, be that completely silent, quiet or with background noise?

11 **Clean and comfortable:** Is furniture modern, clean and comfortable; is food and drink allowed or available (e.g., via vending machines, cafés or other facilities, such as microwaves); is heating appropriate; are there toilets nearby?

12 **Light:** Is the space well lit with natural light? Is there a nice view?

13 **Claimable**: Is there space to spread out and claim it for an extended period of time?

Responses

Welcoming. Sense of belonging was important to students. They had positive feelings towards symbols of the University, such as the University crest. Disciplinary identity also emerged as a stronger factor than expected. Much of the discussion revolved around the Diamond building, which was perceived as being exclusively for engineers through its architecture, interior design and visible practices being carried out there. This created a sense in students from other faculties that it was not for them – 'like I'm intruding,' 'like I've invaded their space' – or even of inferiority (to 'the mighty engineers'), and a realisation that there was no comparable space for their faculty.

Easy to find and navigate. Several commonly used spaces were experienced as hard to navigate, with confusing layout and insufficient signage. Other spaces, such as the Information Commons, were praised because they had consistent, easy-to-understand layouts.

Walkable and convenient. Building usage was heavily influenced by the distance of travel from lecture venues or the student's home. A difference of a few minutes' walk was critical to student choice; but this was sometimes somewhat subjective – some spaces 'just feel further away'. For example, a dual carriageway cutting across the campus did create an extra sense of psychological distance.

Suitable for the task. Although students tended to have a few places they preferred to study in, task did impact choice of place. This is neatly summarised by a questionnaire response: 'Western Bank if I need to focus. IC if I need to work collaboratively. Diamond if I need technical software/hardware.' Some buildings, such as the IC, were liked because they offered options for multiple types of study: 'I use the IC most because it has so many options; comfortable sofas, round tables for group work, closed bookable rooms for more intense work, silent study.' A focus group participant commented: 'If I need to do work around understanding concepts, this is harder to do with people around, [it] can be distracting if you are doing something that needs a lot of concentration.'

Social. As many previous studies have shown, studying alongside others who are friends, even if not on the same course, was valued. Being sent a photo of oneself by a friend, having been spotted in the IC, was a common occurrence. This contributed to a sense of belonging, 'a nice social environment'.

Studious. Going to a suitable place is like a commitment to work: 'Being in the IC makes me feel like I have to work.' Seeing others working was a key aspect of motivation and avoiding distraction.

Connected and resourced. Having USB sockets compatible with a number of devices was often felt to be critical, as well as a plug to keep a laptop charged. Access to university-maintained computers was also an important resource. Students were still influenced to study close to where their subject's books are in the library, although books were mentioned a lot less than digital devices in the questionnaire.

Flexible. A factor that we had anticipated being important, the ability to rearrange furniture to a preferred configuration, was not mentioned. It appeared that students preferred to go to a place that was set up in a desirable way rather than go to spaces where they could reorganise furniture. Yet there were indications that students liked a space that allows for multiple uses, such as talking, studying and eating.

Safe. If anything, students seemed over-trusting that they could leave personal items on desks during breaks. In general, safety seemed to be assumed. Security around late-night study and travelling home was a concern for some: 'at night, in any building, I get very nervous'.

Quiet. Different tasks were seen to require different levels of ambient noise. For some, silence denoted concentration: 'Silence helps me focus.' For others, complete silence was sometimes experienced as oppressive: 'I feel weird going in [silent spaces], feel like I can't move because I'll be making too much noise, it's overly quiet.' The book-centric, traditional Western Bank library was often seen as 'too much', partly for this reason. Students seemed to use music on headphones to block out ambient noise, but also as a motivation and as an aid to concentration. Music offers an important form of control over the study environment.

Clean and comfortable. Comfortable chairs were seen as key to study: 'If the chair's not comfy I'm not going to be productive.' Someone swapping your chair when you take a break seemed to be a recurring problem. Ready access to food and drink was often mentioned. Something as simple as the availability of a microwave for student use had a big impact on student comfort.

Light and having a view. Light was often mentioned as a desirable aspect of space. This was usually expressed as a preference for natural light, but in some cases non-natural light was preferred. Outside views were often mentioned as important, especially those from the Western Bank library, but views within buildings were also important. 'I like the stools on the 4th floor of the IC which look out over the roundabout and the rest of Sheffield. I also like the booths in the Diamond where you can look out into the rest of the building.'

Claimable. Most student study was for an extended period, so it was essential to be able to claim a space: 'Once I've sat down, I don't move … I am here regardless of whatever's going on.' The amount of space that could be fairly claimed and for how long was a cause of potential tension. Having the confidence to ask to share a table that was already partially occupied was also sometimes a problem: 'I'd feel anxious that I was encroaching.' There was disagreement over whether the ability to book individual study spaces was desirable or not. Students found it difficult to navigate digitally to where they could book a space.

The data gives a sense of the rather complex and demanding requirements students had in learning spaces. It was also clear, however, that students were not aware of the wide range of spaces that were available. There was a sense from the data that students tended to pick a few places to study and were not very adventurous in exploring new places. The reliance on just a few favourite spaces could well have been linked to factors such as being easy to find and walkability. However, this became a problem when popular places were busy around examination times. The failure to explore may also have been partly about uncertainty about expected uses. Students often went into spaces for the first time with a sense of being 'daunted': they were not sure what was expected behaviour, or even whether they were allowed to go into these places.

Inclusion

While the list of themes outlined in the previous section perhaps could be taken to suggest a degree of consensus across students in terms of their needs, we were keen in the research to explore differences with a view to learning how to ensure that the campus was in a true sense inclusive.

The focus groups showed a few areas of concern. Fortunately, it did not seem that study spaces were inherently experienced as for men or as 'white'. Feelings of discomfort were more likely to be felt at particular times of day in the context of behaviour such as rowdiness or loud, inappropriate conversations. The safety of leaving campus after studying late into the evening was a particular concern for women.

The focus groups began to reveal more about the needs of disabled students, particularly the sensory overload in certain spaces and the need to feel secure. 'Small' things such as automatic doors that did not work could create great barriers to learning for individuals that might easily go unnoticed by those with the privilege of easy mobility. They wanted better signage for what was on each floor. Building tours were offered at the beginning of the year but this itself could feel too much in the first week. Just entering some buildings could feel overwhelming.

The questionnaire sought to discover more about experiences of difference. Respondents could tick to say they identified with one or more of the categories shown in Table 10.1.

Table 10.1 *Students' identification with difference*

Category	Respondents
BAME	21
LGBTQ+	58
From a working-class background	44
A person with a disability	39
An international student	39
Someone with dependents or major caring responsibilities	4
Having strong religious beliefs	11
None of these things	45

Thus, most respondents identified with at least one of the categories; many ticked more than one. We did not ask about gender. However, it is significant that in the next question only 30 respondents ticked to say they saw a link between these identities and their use of space; 17 said 'maybe'. Thus, a total of only 47/179 (26%) saw any sort of link between social identity and use of space. Most students did not perceive their social identity as shaping their space preferences.

Disabilities
However, it did seem that disability impacted on experience of space. Of students who said 'Yes' to a link between identity and space, 23/30 also said they identified as a person with a disability. And of the 39 people identifying as a person with a disability, 6 also said 'maybe'. Only 10 said 'no'. In contrast, of those identifying as LGBTQ+, 38/58 saw no connection and many of those saying 'yes' also identified as a person with a disability. Thus, it seems the strongest pattern was that disability was shaping a sense of inclusivity in spaces.

The comments provided in a free-text box reinforced the sense that identifying as a person with a disability was the factor most obviously related to use of space. Interestingly, the answers mostly related to neurodiversity and mental health, rather than mobility issues, sight or hearing. As our understanding of disability has broadened, so our understanding of how learning space needs to be designed needs to change significantly.

Within the free-text response, sound levels and crowded spaces were particular issues for many students (a point that was also mentioned in the focus groups):

My mental health issues and (probable) neurodivergence mean I am more averse to crowded spaces than many people.

I am diagnosed with Autistic Spectrum Disorder, and I like a nice quiet place to study without too many people.

I have difficulties with processing auditory information so I can find non-silent study areas overwhelming. I also have social anxiety that makes studying when there's lots of people around difficult – I usually study at the IC 7 am–10 am to avoid the busy periods.

Many of these comments align with traditional expectations of libraries as quiet places in terms both of noise and of people and movement. One comment saw things as being more about balancing different noise levels:

I have anxiety, so I don't like places that are too silent, because I feel like people are gonna notice if I move, nor too busy and loud because too many people give me anxiety.

Another response emphasised the importance of familiarity and continuity:

> Having ADHD makes it hard to study at home as it's easier to get distracted etc. so I appreciate there being lots of choice of study spaces to use. The other thing that autism affects about my choice of study space is that I like familiarity and struggle with change and new environments so I kinda stick to one place to study quite quickly (Western Bank) and only tend to go other places if it's for meeting up with people rather than studying by myself (similarly I wouldn't like studying with other people at Western Bank as it's where I work alone). I wouldn't say being part of the LGBTQ+ community really affects where I study.

Some of those responding would not necessarily identify as having a disability but identified similar issues:

> I don't identify as someone with a disability but I'm going through the process of being diagnosed with ADHD so I get distracted very easily and busy visual/auditory environments make it more difficult for me to focus and get on with work. I don't however feel that my being LGBTQ+ or from a working class background have an effect on my choice of study space.

For some, navigation was an issue:

> I'm autistic and therefore struggle with any other spaces than the students' union as they're really difficult to navigate, I also have Tourette's meaning I struggle with spaces where other people are.

There were just a few responses from students with mobility issues:

> The disabled access in the IC is honestly shocking, the power assisted door is broken so often, and as such I cannot get into the building.

> I struggle with mobility and therefore am more likely to use study spaces close to where I already am (e.g., if I have lectures in the Arts Tower, I will go to Western Bank). I also have autism and ADHD which means I easily get overwhelmed/overstimulated so I find less busy spaces easier to study in (hence my preference for Western Bank rather than the IC). I also find lighting hard to deal with as harsh lighting sets off my sensory overload and makes it very hard to work.

Thus, it was those with forms of disability, especially mental health or neurodiversity, who expressed particular spatial needs. They often shaped demands for quiet auditory and sensory environments and uncrowded places and, for some, also the importance of familiarity and predictability. However, we know that even within the autistic spectrum there is a wide range of needs that we need to understand much better.

Sexual and gender identities

The attentive reader will have noticed that two of these quotes explicitly stated that the author saw no link between LGBTQ+ identities and space preferences. Other comments reiterated this point:

> No, I feel included as an LGBTQ+ woman.

> No, my choices in regard to sitting space when it comes to my sexual identity are more linked towards things internal to me. I feel there are places around campus that accommodate me on my off days just as there are spaces that fit right on better days.

There were a few comments from a LGBTQ+ perspective:

> Being part of a sexual minority, one is always slightly worried at how they are being perceived. Sometimes, if I am not in the mental headspace to steel myself against what I assume people are inevitably thinking, I prefer to study alone.

> Some places don't have gender-neutral toilets and this puts me off going to certain spaces.

Of 21 respondents to the questionnaire identifying as BAME, only four saw a connection between this and choice of study space. The comments of the two each who said 'yes' and 'maybe' implied that disability and cost were the issue, not their ethnicity per se.

Discussion

Although some concerns were raised, overall, the sense was of considerable student satisfaction with the choices of study space available across campus. Students have marked preferences about where they like to study. The selection of space appears to be rather individual, drawing on many interconnected factors, as articulated in the 13 themes outlined above. The list aligns with other attempts to articulate the key features of informal learning spaces, such as in Sodexo (2022). The need for the University to provide a wide range of spaces is therefore underscored. Many factors seem to emphasise the embodied nature of study, with the stress on light, views, sound levels, music, comfort and access to food and drink.

Exploring inclusivity, the main identity-related factors shaping space preferences were mental health and neurodiversity. Disabled students were forthright in asking for uncrowded spaces without sensory overload. This is highly significant for how spaces should be designed. One in five students at Sheffield now have an identified disability. Given the architectural fashion for very open spaces, designed to be highly social and inevitably noisy, it is important to provide other types of space too, which Sheffield does, particularly in the Western Bank library.

Fortunately, students themselves rarely perceived a link between race and LGBTQ+ identity and experiences of informal and social learning spaces. There were hints in our data of issues that need much more in-depth exploration (Crist and Clark/Keefe, 2022). In relation to social class, one student said in the focus group that they felt more comfortable studying in a pub because of its homely, less pressured feel, rather than in the glossy spaces of the Diamond, where they felt imposter syndrome. Fragmentary hints such as this suggest that we need much more qualitative research to explore individual experiences across the diversity of the student body. In a changing social climate, perceptions are evolving rapidly. Such studies would need to be informed by a strong sense of intersectionality: many students identified with multiple minoritised identities. We are only at the beginning of exploring the diversity of needs in learning spaces.

What our data did reveal was that students have to develop quite a complex understanding of the space resources available, including of the complexity that the quality of space varies at different times of day (and at different times in the academic cycle). Such knowledge could be seen as an important but rarely acknowledged dimension of academic literacy. It is an important aspect of student engagement, experience and belonging. Yet our data suggested that students had rather limited knowledge of choices across the campus and that this became critical at times of year when all spaces were in heavy use, such as the examination periods. One emergent practical finding was the need to offer more information about spaces. Students' reluctance to explore was not simply about walkability and convenience but also because many spaces were rather complex to navigate, there was little information about them and they found unfamiliar spaces daunting. This led the project team to think about how to provide more information, such as through a digital campus map annotated with student comments, multimedia downloads to help explain navigation to study rooms or simply QR (Quick Response) codes that linked to live information about each room.

Conclusion

This chapter has examined what students value in study space and whether particular student communities have needs that are not fully satisfied. A demanding list of criteria were developed which help to understand choices students make about where to study. For those designing spaces, we think this list is a useful starting point for analysis. It draws attention away from simple physical dimensions and onto the sensory experiences of spaces (especially aural aspects) and their social feel, and how this can vary at different times of day. Task is important in shaping what space is ideal. It also helps us to remember the importance of access to many resources, including food and drink, less than simply to 'study resources' like books or computers. It prompts us to think beyond architectural models and plans, to acknowledge lived experiences of spaces. We would not wish our list to be used as a checklist but, rather, as a prompt to reflection or discussion with students themselves.

The results were positive in not finding a sense of exclusion among LGBTQ+ or ethnic minority students. We learned quite a lot about the needs of disabled students, especially within our expanding understanding of neurodiversity and mental health as forms of disability. Exploring how students from different perspectives experience the estate will be a future priority in all universities' estates strategies. Many of us involved with space design are very familiar with academic environments and have strong tacit assumptions based on able-bodied or gendered experiences. Even the assumption that we are using a space from 9 am to 5 pm is problematic when we consider the experience of many students, for example, part-time students. An emphasis on trying to imagine the diversity of experiences benefits estates strategy. A continuous conversation with students about their experiences is needed, because we must recognise the shifting nature of expectations.

One important finding that did emerge was the need to provide more information about study spaces. Our study did lead directly to improvements in how information about learning spaces was provided, such as within the Sheffield student app and by providing QR codes in rooms to access timetabling information. In the longer term we hope that the study will support calls for interactive digital mapping of the campus that would assist student navigation and, critically, integrate students' own comments of different spaces. As the management of estate expands beyond emphasis on physical maintenance and towards a greater emphasis on supporting student experience and student voice and ensuring inclusivity, the models offered by libraries of different designs of learning space are of great value. Libraries' efforts over a decade to provide a much greater variety of spaces to support different learning needs provide a model for the campus as a whole.

Our findings are limited by being drawn from a single university at a particular point in time. Some dimensions might be specific to a Russell Group (elite) university. Our focus was on students who studied on campus, and we did not closely examine home conditions of study. There must be a strong interaction between accommodation types and the need for campus space. While we had optimistic findings about the sense of inclusivity of study spaces, there is a need for more studies, as expectations shift and different research methods might elicit a more nuanced picture of experiences, especially as shaped by intersectionality.

References

Allen, L., Cowie, L. and Fenaughty, J. (2020) Safe but not Safe: LGBTTIQA+ Students' Experiences of a University Campus, *Higher Education Research and Development*, **39** (6), 1075–90, https://doi.org/10.1080/07294360.2019.1706453.

Andrews, P. (2016) User Experience Beyond Ramps. In Priestner, A. and Borg, M. (eds) *User Experience in Libraries*, Facet Publishing, https://doi.org/10.4324/9781315548609.

Beilin, I. G. (2017) The Academic Research Library's White Past and Present. In Schlesselman-Tarango, G. (ed.) *Topographies of Whiteness: Mapping Whiteness in Library and Information Science*, Library Juice Press.

Bennett, S. (2009) Libraries and Learning: A History of Paradigm Change, *portal: Libraries and the Academy*, **9** (2), 181–97.

Brook, F., Ellenwood, D. and Lazzaro, A. E. (2015) In Pursuit of Antiracist Social Justice: Denaturalizing Whiteness in the Academic Library, *Library Trends*, **64** (2), 246–84.

Broughton, K. M. (2019) Belonging, Intentionality, and Study Space for Minoritized and Privileged Students, [Paper presentation], ACRL 2019 Conference, Cleveland, Ohio.

Costello, C. Y. (2002) Schooled by the Classroom: The (Re)Production of Social Stratification in Professional School Settings. In Margolis, E. (ed.) *The Hidden Curriculum in Higher Education*, Routledge.

Cox, A. (2017) Space and Embodiment in Informal Learning, *Higher Education*, https://doi.org/10.1007/s10734-017-0186-1.

Cox, A. M. and Benson Marshall, M. (2021) *Drivers for the Usage of SCONUL Member Libraries*, www.sconul.ac.uk/news/research-report-on-drivers-for-the-usage-of-sconul-member-libraries.

Cox, A. M., Benson Marshall, M., Burnham, J. A. J., Care, L., Herrick, T. and Jones, M. (2022) Mapping the Campus Learning Landscape, *Pedagogy, Culture & Society*, **30** (2), 149–67. https://doi.org/10.1080/14681366.2020.1788124.

Crist, E. A. and Clark/Keefe, K. (2022) A Critical Phenomenology of Whiteness in Academic Libraries, *The Journal of Academic Librarianship*, **48** (4), 102557.

Elkington, S. (2019) Future Learning Spaces in Higher Education. In Elkington, S. and Bligh, B. *Future Learning Spaces: Space, Technology and Pedagogy*, AdvanceHE, www.advance-he.ac.uk/knowledge-hub/future-learning-spaces-space-technology-and-pedagogy.

Ellis, S. J. (2009) Diversity and Inclusivity at University: A Survey of the Experiences of Lesbian, Gay, Bisexual and Trans (LGBT) Students in the UK, *Higher Education*, **57** (6), 723–39, https://doi.org/10.1007/s10734-008-9172-y.

Gair, M. and Mullins, G. (2002) Hiding in Plain Sight. In Margolis, E. (ed.) *The Hidden Curriculum in Higher Education*, Routledge.

Gourlay, L. and Oliver, M. (2018) *Student Engagement in the Digital University: Sociomaterial Assemblages*, Routledge.

Halpin (2022) Living Black at University, Unite Students, www.unitegroup.com/living-black-at-university.

Hamilton, L. G. and Petty, S. (2023) Compassionate Pedagogy for Neurodiversity in Higher Education: A Conceptual Analysis, *Frontiers in Psychology*, **14**, 1093290.

Hamraie, A. (2016) Universal Design and the Problem of 'Post-Disability' Ideology, *Design and Culture*, **8** (3), 285–309, https://doi.org/10.1080/17547075.2016.1218714.

Harwood, S. A., Mendenhall, R., Lee, S. S., Riopelle, C. and Huntt, M. B. (2018) Everyday Racism in Integrated Spaces: Mapping the Experiences of Students of Color at a Diversifying Predominantly White Institution, *Annals of the American Association of Geographers*, **108** (5), 1245–59, https://doi.org/10.1080/24694452.2017.1419122.

Jaeger, P. T. (2018) Designing for Diversity and Designing for Disability: New Opportunities for Libraries to Expand Their Support and Advocacy for People with Disabilities, *The International Journal of Information, Diversity, & Inclusion (IJIDI)*, **2** (1/2), https://doi.org/10.33137/ijidi.v2i1/2.32211.

Pionke, J. J. (2017) Toward Holistic Accessibility, *Reference & User Services Quarterly*, **57** (1), 48–56.

Pontoriero, C. and Zippo-Mazur, G. (2019) Evaluating the User Experience of Patrons with Disabilities at a Community College Library, *Library Trends*, **67** (3), 497–515, https://doi.org/10.1353/lib.2019.0009.

Samatar, A., Madriaga, M. and McGrath, L. (2021) No Love Found: How Female Students of Colour Negotiate and Repurpose University Spaces, *British Journal of Sociology of Education*, **42** (5–6), 717–32.

Santamaria, M. R. (2020) Concealing White Supremacy through Fantasies of the Library: Economies of Affect at Work, *Library Trends*, **68** (3), 431–49.

Shaw, J. and Selman, F. (2023) An Asset not a Problem: Meeting the Needs of Neurodivergent Students, Unite students, www.unitegroup.com/neurodivergent-students-report.

Shea, G. and Derry, S. (2019) Academic Libraries and Autism Spectrum Disorder: What Do We Know? *Journal of Academic Librarianship*, **45** (4), 326–31, https://doi.org/10.1016/j.acalib.2019.04.007.

Sodexo (2022) *Social and Informal Learning Spaces*, Association of University Directors of Estates.

Soria, K. M. (2013) Factors Predicting the Importance of Libraries and Research Activities for Undergraduates, *Journal of Academic Librarianship*, **39** (6), 464–70, https://doi.org/10.1016/j.acalib.2013.08.017.

Stevenson, J., O'Mahony, J., Khan, O., Ghaffar, F. and Steill, B. (2019) *Understanding and Overcoming the Challenges of Targeting Students from Under-Represented and Disadvantaged Ethnic Backgrounds*, Office for Students.

Stewart, B. and Kendrick, K. D. (2019) 'Hard to Find': Information Barriers among LGBT College Students, *Aslib Journal of Information Management*, **71** (5), 601–17, https://doi.org/10.1108/AJIM-02-2019-0040.

Tor, D. (2015) *Exploring Physical Environment as Hidden Curriculum in Higher Education: A Grounded Theory Study*, Middle East Technical University.

Watson, L. (2007) Building the Future of Learning, *European Journal of Education*, **42** (2), 255–63.

Wexelbaum, R. S. (2018) Do Libraries Save LGBT Students? *Library Management*, **39** (1–2), 31–58, https://doi.org/10.1108/LM-02-2017-0014.

Whitmire, E., Soria, K. M., Long, D., Harwood, S. A., Mendenhall, R., Lee, S. S., Riopelle, C., Huntt, M. B., Broughton, K. M., Brook, F., Ellenwood, D., Lazzaro, A. E. and Beilin, I. (2011) Everyday Racism in Integrated Spaces: Mapping the Experiences of Students of Color at a Diversifying Predominantly White Institution, *Journal of Academic Librarianship*, **4** (6), 504–11, https://doi.org/10.1080/24694452.2017.1419122.

Conclusion: The Privilege of Working in Partnership

Regina Everitt

What resonates throughout these pages is how essential it is for library and estates and facilities teams to work in partnership to deliver university strategy and to manage any risks to that delivery. In Chapter 1, Black and Kilpatrick discussed safety, business continuity and project risks, and in Chapter 4, O'Neill discussed analysing the risk of not approving or delivering on a business case. Identifying and managing risks to the delivery of university strategy involving libraries and space is the joint responsibility of library and estates leaders. Consider the annual planning cycle for universities. Faculties, schools and services plan how they will contribute to the delivery of university strategy. For example, if the university has a strategy to increase the number of study spaces to accommodate an increase in student numbers, the library leader as key stakeholder will make a useful contribution to any development master plan. Where there are impacts on existing library spaces or development of new spaces, the library and estates leaders will develop a joint business case during the planning cycle. Upon approval of the business case, library and estates leaders will be key players in the governance structure to ensure delivery of the project.

Consider the reopening of buildings as COVID-19 restrictions were lifted. Libraries were among the first buildings to reopen to enable student and staff access to reliable Wi-Fi, personal computers and study spaces. Library teams and estates and facilities teams worked together to implement government guidelines around physical distancing, cleaning protocols and discreet, rapid response to decontamination after reported cases of positive testing. Certainly, at the University of East London, the estates and facilities team was invaluable in enabling the libraries to reopen quickly and safely.

The case studies in this book illustrate how open communication between the library and estates and facilities teams can positively impact on project delivery. The University of Northampton case study by Bradshaw and Powis in Chapter 9, particularly, illustrates how a good working relationship enabled them to deliver an ambitious university strategy.

Lessons learned

So, what are the key lessons learned?

Involve the library leader in master planning. Although the library is an estates asset and, thus, holds no more privilege than any other university building, the library leader must still be involved in university master planning, whether spaces within the libraries are directly impacted or not. It is possible that the change, removal or addition of one space could impact on spaces within the library envelope. For example, limiting or reducing spaces where students can gather socially (e.g., share music, socialise in large groups) may push those activities into library social learning spaces where students may be working collaboratively on course work.

Communicate, communicate, communicate. If there are impending changes in space configuration or service delivery for operational or strategic reasons, the leaders should communicate these as soon as possible in senior leadership meetings and discuss implications. For example, if a new school or faculty requires bespoke spaces or resources, these must be communicated to key stakeholders, including students. An expansion of a game design programme, say, may require additional open access computers with high-quality hardware and software configurations to be available in the library, due to its long opening hours.

Understand roles and expertise. The contributions in this book have aided understanding about the roles, knowledge and expertise within the professions. Although library staff may have site management responsibilities, they may have limited knowledge about regulatory compliance. Although the estates projects team may undertake a post-occupancy evaluation after a new build or major refurbishment, the library team will understand whether the space is being used as planned and if any assumptions need to be challenged.

Future discussions

Although Black and Kilpatrick as well as Everitt, N. (Chapter 6) touched on sustainability, there is much more to be explored around achieving carbon neutrality, smart buildings (e.g., using technology for environmental control) and scope 3 emissions (from institutional supply chain and over which the institution has no control). As discussed in Everitt, R. (Chapter 5), students may factor into their choice of university the institution's stance on environmental sustainability. Is it necessary for university leaders to fly everywhere in order to develop international partnerships, or can technology be leveraged?

Management of smart library buildings is an interesting example of the need for library/facilities management collaboration. There is no shortage of books and articles about *designing* smart buildings, including libraries. However, how well equipped are the library and estates and facilities teams to manage these spaces from day to day? Consider the common concerns that come from student and staff feedback: the library is too hot or too cold; ventilation is poor – COVID-19 is endemic; the lighting sensors don't come on or they turn off too quickly; student attendance is not captured in a lecture theatre. Often, the issue must be reported to some contracted third party with the expertise to sort out the problem; the support for these systems is often out of scope for institutional information technology departments. I am reminded of when my father used to practically rebuild cars by hand, until parts were replaced with electronic 'black boxes' that required vehicles to be sent back to the dealer for what used to be basic repairs, but now at a premium price. Although the rapid advance in technology, particularly artificial intelligence, brings boundless opportunities for environmentally friendly and efficient spaces, library and estates and facilities teams will need to manage user expectations when the building computer says 'no'. However, there are interesting opportunities for the professions to work in partnership to bring innovation into the delivery of university strategy.

Index